RACE RIOTS

New York 1964

RACE RIOTS

New York 1964

FRED C. SHAPIRO

and

JAMES W. SULLIVAN

Thomas Y. Crowell Company

New York, Established 1834

There are some 350,000 residents in the area considered as Harlem, and some 400,000 in what is known as Bedford-Stuyvesant. When things were at their worst in July, no more than 4,000 rioted on the streets of Harlem, and no more than 4,000 in Bedford-Stuyvesant. To the other 742,000 men, women and children who did not let themselves be caught up by their emotions, this book is respectfully—and gratefully—dedicated.

Acknowledgment

The authors would like to express their debt to newspaper and magazine reporters, policemen, social and civil rights workers, and city officials who helped us make this book, and also to Miss Katharine J. Eggers for her typing, editing, and common-sense suggestions which helped them meet a very tough deadline.

Contents

RACE RIOTS

New York 1964

1

Gilligan and Powell

James Powell and Police Lieutenant Thomas R. Gilligan could not have had much less in common and still have been male New Yorkers. Lieutenant Gilligan was a mature white man, thirty-seven years old, a veteran of seventeen years in the Police Department and a resident of a middle-income apartment project on the East Side of Manhattan. Powell was a fifteen-year-old Negro who lived in a lower-income project in the Bronx. At 9:20 A.M. on Thursday, July 16, 1964, they met in front of an apartment house at 215 East 76th Street in that part of New York which is called Yorkville. The policeman's pistol barked. The boy died. And their names became linked, possibly for decades.

The Gilligan-Powell case was the spark which fell into Harlem and, with fire-tending, intentional or unintentional, flamed into the Harlem and Bedford-Stuyvesant riots of 1964.

For six nights, mobs roamed the streets in two boroughs. As many as 4,000 New Yorkers dedicated themselves to attacks on police, vandalism, and looting of stores. When it was all over, police counted 1 rioter dead, 118 injured, and 465 men and women arrested.

And worse, the cause of civil rights had taken one giant step—backwards. The Gilligan-Powell case can be said to have caused the riots which plagued other cities in succeeding weeks, because those riots were patterned on the ones touched off in New York.

Until his pistol spoke in that usually quiet street, Lieutenant Gilligan was a hero cop. He was a handsome, well-built six-footer with a distinguished record. The row of enameled bars which rose in a staggered line above the gold badge on his uniform represented the nineteen citations he had received during his time with the Police Department. Lieutenant Gilligan had shot people before, but had never killed anyone. In 1958, he wrestled a man who was trying to push him off a roof, broke his wrist, and then shot the man as he fled. A few years later a youth who had been looting cars outside Lieutenant Gilligan's apartment in Stuyvesant Town struck him with the heavy nozzle from a fire hose; Lieutenant Gilligan shot him, although two fingers of his gun hand had been broken by the nozzle. The first shooting incident won him the *New York Daily News* Hero Cop award. And he had other citations; four of them for disarming suspects and several for saving lives. He had rescued women and children from a fire, saved an unconscious man by first aid, stopped a man from a suicidal jump, rescued an unconscious man trapped in a basement after an explosion, and used mouth-to-mouth resuscitation to revive a woman who had attempted suicide by swallowing barbiturates. On that fatal July morning in 1964, he was assigned to the 14th Inspection Division in Brooklyn. He was off duty.

2

James Powell lived with his mother, Mrs. Annie Powell, in the Soundview Housing Project. His father, Harold Powell, had died three years before. Neighbors said James was a good boy, but one said he began to get a little wild after his father died. James was a ninth grader at a vocational high school in the Bronx and had been assigned to remedial-reading classes at the Robert F. Wagner, Sr., Junior High School on East 76th Street. Although the Board of Education keeps no racial census on summer classes, most of the students appeared to be Negro. All attended voluntarily. Police said James had had four brushes with the law. Once, he was arrested for an attempted robbery, but he was cleared. Twice he was charged with attempting to board a subway or bus without paying, and once he was charged with breaking a car window. He was beginning to get his growth and stood five feet, six inches and weighed 122 pounds.

James Powell left his home in the Bronx that morning at 7:30 A.M. with two neighbor boys, Clifton Harris, fifteen, and Carl Dudley, fourteen. Cliff Harris said Jimmy had two knives and gave one to each of his friends to be held for him. This later caused the Harris boy considerable trouble at home because his father had forbidden him to have anything to do with knives. The boys traveled to school by subway and were waiting in front of the school for 9:30 classes when they noticed a disturbance across the street.

Patrick Lynch, thirty-six, a short, stocky man who speaks deliberately in the brogue of his native Ireland, is superintendent of three apartment houses across the street from the school and also operates an Irish record shop nearby. Yorkville formerly was a German community, but there are enough Irish immigrants there now to make it

3

worthwhile for newsstands to display the Irish weeklies. Lynch had been having trouble with the summer-school kids.

Among the many details of the fatal incident which are disputed are Lynch's actions of that moment. He was washing down the sidewalk with a hose and there were Negro students sitting on the steps. Lynch said afterward that he asked them to move so they wouldn't get wet when he sprinkled flowers which had been set out on a fire escape above them, but they refused. The students claimed he said: "Dirty niggers, I'll wash you clean," then squirted them. Lynch denies the statement.

At any rate, some of the students seem to have been sprinkled to some degree and they began pelting the superintendent with bottles and garbage-can lids. This was the disturbance which attracted the attention of the three Bronx boys.

It quickly swelled. Lynch ducked inside the apartment building, number 215.

James Powell darted after him. Lieutenant Gilligan, in civilian clothes on his day off, raced out of the neighboring television shop.

James Powell ran back out of the apartment vestibule, confronting Lieutenant Gilligan.

Lieutenant Gilligan fired three shots and Jimmy Powell died on the sidewalk.

This bloody tragedy was acted out in perhaps one minute. It was witnessed by dozens of people.

Did James Powell have a knife in his hand? Did he attack Lieutenant Gilligan?

Cliff Harris said the next day that young Powell had asked Dudley for the knife he had given him. Dudley said he didn't have it. James then asked Cliff for the

4

knife he had given him, and Cliff asked, "What do you want with it?" He said James answered, "Give it to me." Cliff handed it over and James Powell left, saying, "I'll be back." Cliff saw him pass between two parked cars on his way to the apartment house.

On the third floor of the school a French class heard the disturbance, and students and teachers went to the window. A reporter for the *New York Times*, Theodore Jones, talked to them later and thought they may have had the best view of the ensuing tragedy.

The students told him that a man in a white shirt and dark trousers came from the television shop as a Negro boy came out of the vestibule at 215 and down the steps of the apartment building. The man pulled a pistol, and the boy threw up his right arm. They saw no knife in the boy's hand and thought the gesture was defensive, as if to hold the man off. The gun barked when the boy and the man were about four feet apart, the boy kept moving —the watchers thought because of momentum—and the gun fired again and again and the boy fell to the sidewalk.

Like the French students, most of the witnesses gave versions that varied considerably, even to the spacing of the shots. Some said there were two fast shots, a pause, and then another shot.

Cliff Harris, located and interviewed the next day, remembered a single shot, then two more. He looked across the street and saw two girls running and his friend James Powell lying on the ground.

"I ran over to where he was and got down on my knees next to him and said, 'Jimmy, what's the matter?'" he said.

James Powell didn't answer. Cliff saw him start to spit blood, saw the man standing over him with a gun, and asked the man if he shouldn't call an ambulance. He says the man answered, "No, this black ——— is my prisoner. You call an ambulance." Cliff ran to the corner candy store.

Mrs. Beulah Barnes, a housewife and nurse, told Jones she had seen the shooting and described it in simple terms:

"I saw the superintendent spraying a bunch of colored kids and as the kids moved back he went after them with more water. Then someone threw an empty soda bottle and then another bottle. Then the man went into the building and then a colored boy ran after him. The boy didn't stay two minutes. Then this tall man with black hair came out of the radio shop and he had a little black revolver. I saw that. As the boy came out, he shot him twice and then the boy fell to the sidewalk and this man stood there for maybe ten minutes just staring at the body. The boy never had any words with the man."

Lieutenant Gilligan had fired three shots. One had gone through a pane of glass in the door of the apartment house; another had gone through James Powell's right forearm near the wrist, then tore into his chest, cutting the main artery just above the heart and stopping in the lungs; the third had gone through his abdomen and out his back. An autopsy showed that the chest wound would have been fatal under almost any circumstances, but the pathologist thought the youth might have been saved if he had suffered only the abdominal wound and had been gotten to a hospital quickly. Police later pointed to the forearm-chest wound as indicating that the hand had been raised in position for a knife thrust.

Max Francke, principal of the summer school, told there was trouble outside, went out, saw the dead youth on the sidewalk, and returned to tell his secretary to call an ambulance. Police arrived and found a crowd of students gathered around. They ordered them to the other side of the street and the crowd went. The students then came back across the street and police ordered them away again. They obeyed. A third time, the students edged across the street and police shooed them away. But a news service photographer had arrived and climbed atop a car for a picture. His arrival influenced what happened next. The students were grieving openly, many of the girls crying. Suddenly, one of the girls cried, "Come on, shoot another nigger!" and the emotion erupted into action.

Garbage-can lids, bottles, and rocks began to fly, and crying girls ran back and forth in the street, while the principal and teachers begged the students to quiet down. Police brought in seventy-five steel-helmeted reinforcements, who quietly pushed the students away from the scene. In the midst of the turmoil, a bottle felled a Negro patrolman. Police action drew a tribute from *Herald Tribune* reporter Sue Reinert, who had covered civil rights disturbances before. "The police were very nice, I must say," she said later. "Of course, most of the troublesome ones were girls."

At the peak of the disturbance, about three hundred students were involved, but it ended without a fight and without any arrests. Police took three hysterical girls into custody but released them after they calmed down.

Police reports were sketchy. Lieutenant Gilligan was taken away to Roosevelt Hospital for treatment of an arm injury suffered in the affair, then was taken to the precinct and whisked through with only the briefest questioning by the one reporter who happened to see him.

The problem was that most of the teen-age witnesses

7

had been greatly influenced by their emotions. Francke said that, of three girls who told him they had seen the shooting, two certainly had not and the third might have seen it.

The grand jury which spent nearly a month and a half investigating the case complained of a similar problem. When, on September 1, 1964, it refused to indict Lieutenant Gilligan, District Attorney Frank Hogan released a fourteen-page summary of testimony and emphasized the conflicts in the testimony. The witnesses could not agree on how the two confronted each other or what Powell had in his hand; some said his hand was empty, some said he had a knife, some said he had a beer can.

"According to the most frequent account, after Powell fell to the sidewalk on his hands and knees, the officer, still on the steps, pointed the gun down on him and fired two more shots at Powell's back," the report said. (See Appendix for text of the District Attorney's report.)

The conflict here was with physical evidence. The autopsy testimony said the shots entered the front of his body and added, "the absence of any impact marks on the newly cemented sidewalk negated any possibility that Powell had been shot in the abdomen while lying on the ground." Because of the absence of powder burns, the report said, a ballistics expert believed the gun must have been "farther than two feet from Powell's body when fired."

Lieutenant Gilligan's version of what really happened did not come out until it was released in the report of District Attorney Hogan. The officer's story—unanimously upheld in the grand jury's vote not to indict—is basically that, after hearing the crash of broken glass, he stepped outside the television service store and found Powell running toward the building yelling, "Hit him, hit him, hit him." Gilligan did not see Lynch, but he did see, in Powell's right hand, an open knife.

Gilligan took his badge from his left trouser pocket, his revolver from his right, and moved to a point facing the building entrance. There he says he yelled, "I'm a police lieutenant. Come out and drop it."

Instead, the officer says, Powell turned, raised the knife, and lunged. Gilligan then fired the warning shot and again told Powell to stop. When the youth lunged for the second time, Lieutenant Gilligan says, he blocked it with his gun hand, and the knife scraped his arm.

Lieutenant Gilligan said Powell lunged yet another time. That is when he fired the bullet which deflected off Powell's forearm and into his chest. When Powell still kept coming, the lieutenant said, he stepped back and fired his third and final shot into the youth's midsection.

But the official report on the shooting was not issued until six long weeks after James Powell died and, on that hot July day, the people of New York got the versions that reporters were able to ferret out for them.

In the highly charged scene on East 76th Street, some of the students shouted that Lieutenant Gilligan had kicked the boy after he fell to the sidewalk, others said he had lifted him with his foot. Many of the students insisted that Powell had not carried a knife.

Shirley Robinson, a fourteen-year-old student, was among those who denied that Powell was armed.

"I saw the boy go into the building and he didn't have any knife then," she said. "When he came out, he was even laughing and kind of like running and then the cop was on the street going into the building and then he shot him, then twice more and then when he was on the ground, turned him over with his foot."

Police, dribbling out information, first said the youth

was five feet, seven inches tall and weighed 175 pounds, but the coroner's report showed him to be much lighter.

Newsmen had to make do with a secondhand, obviously incomplete, version retailed by Deputy Chief Inspector Joseph Coyle. A public statement by Lieutenant Gilligan the day of the shooting might have taken some of the steam out of the trouble that was to come, but Lieutenant Gilligan was under wraps, and was to remain there until the grand jury finished its investigation.

But the children at the site of the shooting were not going to wait for the grand jury. They finally were cleared out of the block under the encouragement of police and stormed into Lexington Avenue, still highly charged with emotion. A large group went into the 77th Street entrance of the IRT Lexington Avenue subway station, leaped over the turnstiles, raked newspapers and magazines off a newsstand counter onto the platform, and banged on the doors of a train. When the white motorman didn't open the doors, one of them pulled a screwdriver from his pocket and slashed at him as the motorman rode past. Upstairs, on the street level, a group, mostly girls, blocked the sidewalk as they talked excitedly about the slaying. A white woman tried to push her way through them, and one of the girls shouted, "What do you think you're doing?" and slapped her. She crossed the street. A woman in a flower shop at the intersection said some of the teen-agers had hurled a flower pot through her window and cursed her. She was terrified. At 76th Street, a group of Negro girls was telling a white policeman, "Don't get us mad." A tall Negro girl walked past, weeping and shouting, "Don't let him go free!" in apparent reference to Lieutenant Gilligan.

To the Congress of Racial Equality this tragic incident was another example of "police brutality." It buttressed

CORE's campaign for a civilian board to review charges of unnecessary use of force by police. Three representatives of CORE, including Blyden Jackson, a field secretary of the national organization, and two members of the East River chapter, had appeared on the scene, looked it over, and were holding an impromptu press conference for television cameras and microphones at 77th Street and Lexington Avenue. They said they suspected this was an unnecessary killing and that it emphasized the need for the civilian review board.

They said they would recommend that a group outside the Police Department investigate this shooting. *Herald Tribune* reporter Reinert asked them if they would consider a grand jury investigation satisfactory, and they said they would. Like most people, they did not seem to realize that all killings by policemen in New York are investigated by a grand jury to see if they were justifiable.

Police now announced that a knife had been found near the body. School principal Francke said a teacher had found a knife in the gutter about eight feet from the youth's body and had told him about it.

When the turmoil ended, twenty-five policemen remained on duty around the vicinity of the school. Some of the merchants complained that they had been having constant trouble with the summer-school students and closed their establishments early to avoid them. Others in the neighborhood also complained about the students.

Francke was inclined to blame the entire incident, including the little riot, on Lynch. The racial overtones were produced because a white adult didn't use his good sense.

"What could have been handled very promptly and efficiently by the school turned into a tragedy," he said.

He and Lynch, it developed when Mrs. Reinert later

11

interviewed the superintendent, had been at odds for some time. Lynch agreed with the merchants that the summer-school students were troublesome. He said he and his tenants had complained repeatedly to school authorities about the students littering the sidewalks and stoops of the apartment houses and that he also had registered more than twenty complaints with police, none of which had been answered.

"The other day, my wife was on the street when a couple of kids went for each other with bottles," he said. "My wife went upstairs and called the police, but they never came. They always come after something serious. But why couldn't they come before? Then this would never have happened."

The week before, Lynch said, the owner of one of the apartment houses he tended had gathered up the litter on her stoop and left it in a bag on Francke's desk. "He threw her out of the school—that's the kind of principal he is," said Lynch, bitterly.

The superintendent said regular-session students at the school were "friends of mine."

"They sit on my stoops to eat lunch and I don't pass any remarks. They clean up. They're good kids."

Board of Education figures showed that the normal enrollment of the school was 26 percent Negro, 26.3 percent Puerto Rican, and 47.7 percent white.

The next day, Friday, CORE demonstrated.

About seventy-five demonstrators showed up at the school at 8 A.M. and began to parade in front of it. About fifty policemen appeared, carrying nightsticks. This equipment, unusual on daytime assignment, was protested and, after conferences with a representative of the City Com-

12

mission on Human Rights, the clubs were sent back to the precinct. The policemen remained. By noon, there were more than two hundred pickets in front of the school, many of them students. They started a chant which was to become very familiar in the next week: "Killer cops must go!" Their signs included, "STOP KILLER COPS! . . . WE WANT LEGAL PROTECTION . . . POLICE BRUTALITY MUST GO . . . DEMANDAMUS EL FIN DE BRUTALIDAD POLICIACA [sic] . . . END POLICE BRUTALITY." Several of the pickets were whites and Puerto Ricans.

At noon, they started a march to the 19th Precinct on East 67th Street, which had not been involved in the shooting the day before, but which was police headquarters for the area. Police would not let them all picket in front of the station because of the probable inconvenience to the nearby firehouse, the Russian Mission to the United Nations, and the Kennedy Child Study Center, but they permitted a token force of twenty-five pickets to enter the block. The rest paraded on 67th Street between Lexington and Park Avenues, to the wonderment of students at the Lexington School for the Deaf, who came out, stared, and discussed the demonstration in sign language.

As the demonstration ended, the teen-agers gathered around television cameras and told the reporters how angry they were. Then, three of Malcolm X's dissident group of Black Muslims showed up at the scene and began to question the youngsters about the slaying, urging them not "to let people push you around." The Progressive Labor Movement, Harlem-based and Peking-oriented, had representatives present. A fifteen-year-old boy who said he was from Monroe, N.C., was passing out PLM leaflets. In Monroe, he said, "if the cops shoot a Negro, we arm ourselves and get that cop worse than he got us."

13

This was alarming talk. A man who said he was from CORE told the youngsters that the situation was different in Monroe, holding that authorities there officially perpetuated racism, while in New York "not all police are racists, although racists predominate."

CORE officials urged the students to picket the school every day until young Powell's funeral (the date had not been set yet) and then to "empty the school" and go to the services.

They also told the students that police and reporters were expecting them to be as disorderly on the way home as they had been the day before. Chris Sprowal, chairman of Downtown CORE, discouraged this. "We're going to fool them," he said. "We're going to act like what we are—young ladies and gentlemen."

It didn't quite work out that way. As the demonstrators headed for the subway to go to their homes, a man passing by noted their signs and shouted, "He deserved killing!" The pickets started for him, but police got there first and hustled him behind the police barrier, where *he* was strongly urged to go home. Reporters asked his name, which he refused to give, but he volunteered some thoughts. "What the hell business do they have carrying knives?" he asked. "What was the cop supposed to do—stand there and get stuck?"

Meanwhile, New York was having subway troubles again and was inclined to blame them on the emotional outburst attending the shooting of the boy.

A fifty-one-year-old Yonkers pharmacist, riding an IRT express downtown through the Bronx, was beaten by six Negro youths and robbed of $100 and his wristwatch. About fifteen adults and twenty other youths were in the car, but, as usual, no one offered him any help, although he said, "I yelled plenty."

14

About the same time, Julian Zalewski, a fifty-seven-year-old actor, came from Columbia Presbyterian Hospital, where he had been treated for glaucoma, and boarded an IND train at 125th Street and St. Nicholas Avenue. He said later that he noticed eight or nine Negro youths dropping watches and money into a cloth pouch held by a girl and then, as the train pulled out of the station, the youths threw him to the floor, beat him, and robbed him of $26.

That station is in Harlem and it figured. Whenever a racial fuse is lighted in New York City, the explosion—large or small—can be expected to take place uptown.

2

The Tensions of Harlem

One of the two Negro members of the grand jury which refused unanimously to indict Lieutenant Gilligan was seventy-year-old George S. Schuyler, New York editor of the *Pittsburgh Courier,* and a proclaimed Barry Goldwater conservative.

Mr. Schuyler is proud of the grand jury report. "I did the right thing and so did the rest of the jury," he said. "We heard everything and we're more expert on the subject because we were there. I've been on juries for the last twenty years and so I think I know what I'm talking about."

Another thing Mr. Schuyler is proud of is his race. His wife is a Texas-born white woman of Irish descent and proud of it. Their daughter, Philippa, thirty, is a former child prodigy of whose brains any race could be proud. She could read when she was two years old, started school at the age of three, and is now a noted pianist and authoress. They live with other upper-crust Negro families in an apartment house on Convent Avenue.

In another section of Harlem, in a tenement long since condemned, there lives a Negro woman who has nine children under her care, the eldest a seventeen-year-old girl, the youngest a baby. Eight of the children are hers, although she has never been married. The youngest is the son of her fourteen-year-old daughter, who is not married. Everybody in the household has venereal disease. The older girls have told of repeatedly helping to provide sexual entertainment for their mother's friends. They live on welfare, which also would find decent housing for them, except that the mother-grandmother likes the privacy of her present living quarters and refuses to move. These frightful circumstances would seem to make an ironclad case for legal action to remove the children from their mother's custody. The New York City Welfare Department went to court and came away crushed. The judge had ruled that, because of the obvious affection shown by the children, he could not separate them from their mother.

The Schuylers may not be the height of Harlem and the woman in the condemned house may not be the depth, but they are near the two poles of Harlem society. Between them, living at various latitudes which grow considerably more crowded as you approach the woman in the condemned building, about 200,000 Negroes are stacked in a three-and-a-half-square-mile area at the rate of 200 to the acre.

The words "Negro" and "Harlem" are so closely associated that it comes as a shock to learn that, in the history of Harlem, the Negro is a newcomer.

Nieuw Haarlem was founded by Peter Stuyvesant more than a century before the Revolutionary War and was a farming community until the last century was well under way. It was pleasant and pastoral, lying in a small valley

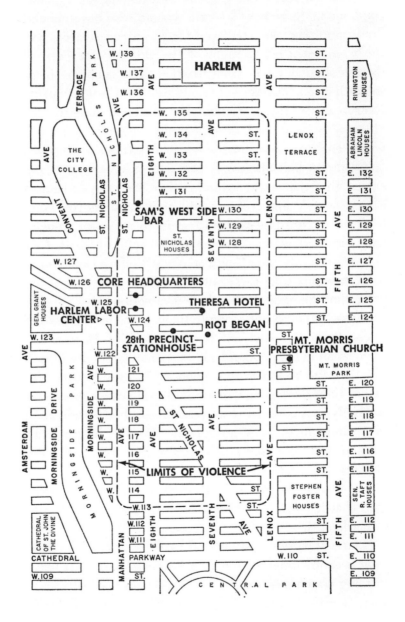

between the East River and Morningside Heights, and traces of its former beauty still remain in Morningside Park and Mount Morris Park. In the last century, it was joined to New York City and, when the elevated railway was extended there after the Civil War, it became a fashionable place in which to live and also in which to invest. The land boom which started then was eventually to concentrate the Negro in Harlem.

The Negroes had been moving uptown since their security was shattered downtown by the draft riots of 1863, but they were confined mostly to such areas as Hell's Kitchen on the West Side, which was predominantly Irish. Negroes wanted to live in Harlem, that sparkling community of upper-middle-class townhouses, but Harlem was very busy keeping them out. It was not until the real-estate bubble burst shortly after the turn of the century that fortress Harlem fell to the blacks. Even then, it was long becoming entirely Negro.

Deputy Inspector Casimir Kruszewski, who was in command of the 28th Precinct at the time of the 1964 riots, was born in Harlem and remembers that in 1926 "no more than two out of ten of the people who passed you on 116th Street were Negroes." His family moved to Queens that year, not because the Kruszewskis objected to the Negroes, but because of the Italians who were moving into the neighborhood. "I whipped this kid fair and square," he recalls, "but his two big brothers caught me and held me while he beat me, so we moved."

By that time, there were enough Negroes in Harlem to form an identifiable and even a glamorous culture. As a center for Negroes, Harlem also became a center for jazz, which was finding many devotees among whites. Nightclubs sprang up which catered to whites only and pro-

19

vided top jazz performances by such notables as Duke Ellington and Louis Armstrong. The Negro ferment began. There was Father Divine, Sweet Daddy Grace, Marcus Garvey, and a host of others preaching various kinds of salvation to the Negro—payment in advance, of course. Harlem became the big time, not only for Negroes with legitimate talent, but also for any confidence man or quack philosopher with a dark skin. With the night life and heavenly life and quackery, there was Depression poverty, squalor, "rent party" high life, and brilliant, introspective youngsters pondering their plight and trying to arrive at philosophic solutions or rationalizations for their problems.

Even in this Golden Age, it was a turbulent area, which could erupt into disorder during any given hot summer day. In 1935, a Negro boy attempted to steal a penknife from a store. Clerks grabbed him, but he slipped away from them before he could be arrested. The story that spread through Harlem was that he had been beaten to death, and the emotional volcano erupted. When the dust settled, there were four dead, about one hundred injured, and property damage was estimated at a million Depression dollars.

In August, 1943, a white policeman attempted to arrest a woman for disorderly conduct in a Harlem hotel. A Negro military policeman who was in the hotel on leave interfered. The MP took the policeman's nightstick from him and felled him with it. The policeman answered the blow with a bullet in the MP's shoulder. The rumor that spread through Harlem was that the policeman had killed the soldier.

There was an important but never-voiced point to the resultant riot. Northern Negroes drafted into the Army were making what was often their first incredulous acquaintance with segregation. Many had been sent to camps in the South, where some refused, after a bad experience, to accept passes to town; but worst of all was the segregation then official within the Army, which reduced them completely to second-class status. Anger over the Army's discriminatory treatment of Negro soldiers was high in Harlem, and so was the toll of the riot which erupted that night. It left six persons dead, five hundred injured, and an estimated million dollars in property damage—all accomplished in a single night.

The postmortems on that riot ignored the real grievance about Negro citizen-soldiers. The mob's fury was blamed on discrimination in employment and on a lack of playgrounds.

Modern Harlem was born in World War II. The nightclubs which had catered to whites only died. Some good jazz spots remained, but they accepted people of any race, and Harlem never became quite as fashionable an entertainment spot as it had been before the war. The wartime influx of Southern Negroes—many of them recruited at home for the manpower-hungry North—crowded nearly all the remaining white residents out of Harlem. Whites still came there for entertainment, but now it was vice that drew them—narcotics and prostitution.

And integration, of all things, damaged Harlem. Since the war, it has been possible for upper-class Negroes to move to one of the suburbs in Westchester County, Long Island, or Connecticut. Many of them have moved and with them has gone much of Harlem's stability. Jackie Robinson, an important Negro voice, lives in Connecticut.

Physically, Harlem is rather difficult to define, since it is not a governmental entity. There is a tendency to say it includes all the Negro neighborhoods in the upper part of Manhattan. Harlem Youth Opportunity Unlimited (HARYOU), the agency which has been given $117 million to further its plans for uplifting the community, likes to speak of Central Harlem, which is bounded by Third Avenue on the east, 110th Street on the south, a string of parks on the west, and the Harlem River on the northeast. There are nearly 200,000 human beings in this three-and-a-half-square-mile area, almost all of them Negroes.

Spiritually, Harlem's boundaries are much wider. It exists in the heart of nearly every American Negro. It is the capital of his world, Nob Hill to all the Negro communities which exist as other worlds in nearly all American cities. It's the Negro Broadway, center of the Negro intellect, center of Negro fermentation. In a cruder age, before such terms as wop, dago, kike, polack, mick, and nigger went out of style, it was known as "Nigger Heaven."

The business places stretching continuously along 125th Street are not Fifth Avenue types, but they are clean and glittering and would be a credit to several streets in downtown Toledo or Detroit. The jazz played in some of the nightspots is big time. Some of the people walking the streets are big time—athletes, entertainers, civil rights leaders; even, sometimes, Harlem's congressman, the Reverend Adam Clayton Powell.

From the streets, Harlem is by no means completely ugly. Its avenues are little valleys which run between five- and six-story buildings. Canyons run off them as narrow side streets, but are quickly broken by another valley. The sun can be seen when it shines.

Harlem once offered the finest in housing in New York City and many of those fine old homes are still there, standing mockeries of their former glory. New York's

22

brownstones were built tough, and many of those in Harlem have stood decades of abuse. Even today, they don't look bad from the street.

"The outsides are pretty," says a glum Negro, "but take a look inside."

Outside, there may be a nice finish to the house, with nothing to mar its appearance except the windows, some of them broken, some of them showing ragged curtains. Inside, the plaster is falling, wires are exposed, stairs are dangerously shaky, garbage litters the halls, the basement may be filled with water which threatens the foundations, and rats may retreat slowly and defiantly before an intruder. These are rooming houses. Entire families of five or six live in each room, sharing one bath and one kitchen on each floor.

These are the houses which bring tenants flocking to the banner of Jesse Gray when he proposes a rent strike against the landlords who are unwilling or unable to repair them.

There is adequate housing in Harlem, some of it in carefully maintained brownstones, whitestones, and apartment buildings; but most of it is in city, state, and Federally financed projects, which rear their sheer sides in several locations, lacking the grace of the older homes, but offering grass, open areas, modern facilities, and interior elbow room.

There also is excellent housing in Harlem in some of the apartments along Convent Avenue, on Sugar Hill, and in Strivers' Row, the brownstones designed by Stanford White. These handsome homes were the first Harlem residences for Negroes and are still well maintained by people who live comfortably. There also is middle-income public housing and more of it coming.

It is the people who make Harlem what it is: the American Negroes, with all their virtues, vices, complexes, and problems.

The Theresa Hotel, at the corner of Seventh Avenue and 125th Street, is a second-rate hotel by nearly any standards. Integration in New York has progressed to the point where anyone with the price of a room can register at any of the big hotels in mid-town Manhattan, regardless of the color of his skin. But big-name Negroes still register at the Theresa because, they say, they feel in Harlem that they "belong."

A belligerent Harlem resident will announce that he owns Harlem, though in the next breath he may be railing against the absentee white businessmen and landlords who do own the glittering stores on 125th Street, the bars on Lenox Avenue, and the noisome tenements on the side streets. He means that he is at home in Harlem, and his meaning becomes clear when you hear the loud jazz coming from the United House of Prayer for All People on the second floor of a building at the corner of Eighth Avenue and 125th Street, see the young men twisting all alone in a doorway to the music blaring from a phonograph in a record shop on 125th Street, hear the curbstone orators denouncing the "blue-eyed white devil" at Seventh Avenue, catch a hostile eye rolled at your pale skin from their audience, and hear the obscenities dropping like flakes of soot from casual conversations on streets or in bars.

Even an integrated Negro feels the pull of Harlem. A Negro reporter, educated, respected by whites for his skill, who has never worked for any but a general circulation publication and who moves freely in the white world, says that he feels more relaxed in Harlem. "You feel as though no one is looking at you," he explains.

Harlem is where the Negro's voice is multiplied a hundred thousand times, where people listen to him, where the white man is not looking over his shoulder, where he can drop the inhibitions he assumes in the white world. It is the cultural center (in the sociological sense) which many white Americans find when they visit the lands of their ancestors—England, France, Italy, Scotland, Germany, Ireland, Israel, Greece, or wherever they sprang from. Probably it's more pronounced in the Negro, whose skin color and culture (again in the sociological sense) have made him the most alien of all the immigrant stocks which populate the United States.

Certainly Harlem contains some people who are fine by any but the most bigoted standards. Police are quick to point this out.

There are rich people in Harlem. A. A. Austin, the real-estate man who once was known as the wealthiest man in Harlem, is dead, but his three sons still live in the community. There are magazine and newspaper editors. There are people as respectable and conservative as any Midwestern bank president. Mr. Schuyler is one of the few Negro Goldwater supporters. There are doctors, lawyers, dentists, and bank officials in Harlem—not enough of them, but they are there.

There are social workers, post office employees, clerks, office managers, nurses, and stenographers, many of whom live as well as their white counterparts. Again, however, there are not enough of them.

There are fine, law-abiding citizens in every economic stratum, including the very poor.

There are entirely too many poor people. No one knows for sure how many of the people of Harlem are supported by the Welfare Department. The community is divided among three offices, all of which cover other areas besides Harlem. HARYOU's thick report estimates that 22.6 percent of the children in Harlem are supported by the Aid to Dependent Children program. Guesses at the number of Harlemites receiving welfare benefits range from an admittedly conservative 10 percent to a probably too high 25 percent. It is certain that the welfare program is a basic part of Harlem's economy.

HARYOU's now-famous report includes a transcript of sample complaints spoken by Negroes into a tape recorder. They are so many and varied that it is tempting to decide that Negroes are simply whiners, but even the most superficial look at their condition shows that they have some very real problems.

Welfare workers feel the biggest problems are unemployment and illegitimacy.

Unemployment stems from racial discrimination, low educational levels, and, most important of all, automation. The vast bulk of Harlem's working people are service workers. Every new automatic elevator, coin-operated food-vending machine, and floor-scrubbing machine takes jobs from unskilled workers, and those workers are very apt to be Negroes, who, generally, are the last to be hired and the first to be fired. James R. Dumpson, the able Negro who heads the New York Department of Welfare, says the bulk of the 20,000 jobs lost to automation in the United States each week are lost by Negroes.

In addition, Harlem has thousands of persons working full time at salaries lower than the amount the Welfare Department would provide for their families if they were unemployed. These families receive supplementary welfare benefits, plus carfare, lunch money, and union dues. The trouble is that the wage-earner must bring home every cent of his pay to keep the budget out of trouble. If he spends a dollar in a bar, there likely will be a family fight, which may conclude with the wife realizing that she would be better off without a wage-earner and the husband realizing that his departure would not make any difference in the family's income, since the Welfare Department would increase the benefits. This, welfare workers believe, accounts for some of Harlem's many deserting fathers.

Conscious that many of the welfare cases are immigrants from the South, Dumpson puts up an argument for Negro civil rights in the South which would appeal to the most bigoted Northern taxpayer. If the Southern Negro could vote, he says, he would be important enough for the Southern politician to provide him with education and welfare benefits, and he would not make the trek north, arriving hungry and unskilled to burden welfare departments in New York, Detroit, Chicago, and other cities.

But the problem which irritates social workers most is illegitimacy. It seems so unnecessary. They don't put the blame exclusively on the women. One worker speaks with restrained venom of a group of men who can be found at any time around one of the Lenox Avenue intersections. "They boast of how many babies they have by women in the rooming houses around there," he says. "It's a personality disease. There should be some sort of treatment for it and we should be able to get them treated."

A female worker shows more compassion, although she remembers with disgust a man who was named by five women as the father of their babies, all born within a few months of each other. "There are so many idle men here," she says. "You see them all up and down Lenox Avenue."

The idle man is a tough problem in Harlem. The Negro

27

woman has always been more acceptable to whites and can nearly always find work as a domestic. The man meets suspicion and fear. The result, since the woman is the dependable bread-winner of the family, is a matriarchal society, which many authorities blame for the surprising amount of homosexuality in Harlem.

But illegitimacy's worst aspect is that it tends to continue into succeeding generations. "We've got to find some way of breaking this chain of illegitimacy," says Mrs. Magda Luft, head of the Central Harlem welfare office.

Harlem's youth does not get the same education as children in better neighborhoods. The school plants are old and sometimes very dilapidated, and teachers in the junglelike classrooms are often too frightened to do more than stand near the door and try to keep the students quiet. The civil rights groups maintain that transporting the children to other schools will solve the problem, but some doubt that these children—like any slum children, with their peculiar problems—are fitted to absorb education by standard teaching methods. Some are so accustomed to screening out the various sounds in their crowded, noisy quarters that they cannot catch nuances in words. Most have no encouragement at home and find it impossible to study there, even if they feel so inclined. Educators are experimenting with such things as a prekindergarten program to prepare slum children for learning, and they have some hope that it will work.

The progress made in the care of the poor since the 1930's is very evident in Harlem. The infant mortality rate may be double that of the rest of the city, but there are no apparent victims of malnutrition and there are few ragged children. In fact, on a sunny Sunday afternoon, Harlem is a pretty community. Its residents are dressed in their best, the processed hair of the women gives evidence of money spent on personal appearance; the nonrespectable element is still sleeping off the previous night's excesses and the sun brings out the warm tones built into once-good buildings. It is hard, watching the Negro children skip rope or play stickball in the streets, to believe the man who says that these are among the toughest streets in Harlem.

His truthfulness becomes apparent at night, when the prostitutes, the junkies, the muggers, the winoes, and the brawlers appear on the lower part of Lenox Avenue and the white Johns cruise by in their cars to select a woman and maybe to contribute to the illegitimacy problem. Now, Harlem is obviously a different world, one which, with a few differences in such superficialities as complexion and costume, could be painted by Hogarth. This is a dark England of Industrial Revolution days, with the gin flowing and, worse still, the narcotics moving as fast as the male junkies can steal and rob and the females can prostitute themselves to obtain the money to feed their habit.

Life is not expensive here. The homicide rate is six times as high as the average for New York City. Policemen at the precinct level will tell you that the murder of a Negro by a Negro costs the offender about eighteen months at most. A nonfatal slash of a knife, which is more frequent, costs much less.

This is the world the police know, where rape and assault and murder and theft and addiction are a part of life, where teen-agers get hooked on narcotics, where a man's life can be ended at any moment by the darting of an arm from the shadows, where there seem to be no rules, no discipline, nothing but a vast, heaving anarchy.

And, still, there are good people here. Weaving through even these crowds are decent citizens who are there from force of circumstances and wish they weren't. Also weaving around are the innocents: the children who didn't ask to be born and, more especially, didn't ask to be born black, but who are now semiorphans in Harlem. They can't be written off, because some of them will survive this situation. Welfare workers like to tell of the sullen seventeen-year-old unwed Negro mother who was brought to them from one of the rooming houses. She had been raped when she was thirteen and had had a rough life since. An IQ test startled everyone. Her IQ was 150. She has been put with a good family, entered in school and is doing well.

In fact, if you believe police at the precinct level, a lot of these children will become fairly stable citizens. It's a firm belief there that 90 percent of the people arrested in Harlem were born somewhere else, usually in the South. "The only New York-born Negroes we arrest are usually connected with the numbers game," says one ranking officer.

Everyone dismisses numbers with the comment that "it's a way of life in Harlem." Estimates of the number of Harlemites who wager a small sum on their favorite three-digit combination run as high as 100,000 daily. The right combination pays high odds, but not as high as the odds against hitting it. Dream books are available at nearly any newsstand to tell you what numbers to bet if you dream of certain things.

If 100,000 people play the numbers each day, the activity should be evident to police, who should be able to slow it down. Negroes insist that police are paid off by the white men who make fortunes on the numbers business.

They go further and charge that police are paid to lay off of narcotics and prostitution.

Police Commissioner Michael J. Murphy, whose men, as this is written, are being investigated by two grand juries for connections with bookmakers, grows heated when the latter charge is repeated to him. "We have our faults," he says, "but I don't know of anyone who takes money from narcotics or prostitution. I don't know of any policeman who wouldn't despise a man who did that."

Yet, prostitution and narcotics flourish in Harlem, even though narcotics peddling is one of the few illegal acts which brings a protest from nearly everyone who lives there. All protest that it wrecks youngsters' lives.

These are volatile people who live in Harlem. The American Negro can often be distinguished from the Caribbean Negro by his lack of ease, the tension that is obvious in him. That tension seems to spring from racial discrimination and to be magnified by the conditions of poverty. Few organizations in Harlem try to relax the Negro; many tend to wind him even tighter.

The home institutions in Harlem are the churches—418 of them, including 296 in store fronts, theaters, or brownstones, in the three-and-one-half-square-mile area—the civil rights organizations, the nationalist groups, and the political groups. There are an amazing number of charlatans and crackpots in these groups.

The 418 churches would appear to be a great deal of religion, but too much of it is "Jesusology," a frank stirring of the emotions to an immoderate pitch with no demand for more discipline, preached all too often by an untrained minister. Police say that, just as there are diploma mills in the United States, there are "holy order mills," which will not only ordain a minister, but even consecrate a bishop by mail for $25. Under these circumstances, it is not surprising that many Negroes have a contempt for religion. Too often, the brand they have seen is ridiculous, like the people who offer it.

The most influential groups in Harlem today, besides the genuine churches, appear to be the civil rights organizations and the Muslims. Of these groups, only the Urban League and the National Association for the Advancement of Colored People have any lengthy history. They have been in the van of the fight for Negro rights for decades, but both have been dedicated to legal battles and persuasion and their thunder has been largely stolen by the activist groups, such as the Congress of Racial Equality.

The New York chapter of CORE is aggressive, militant. Its membership includes young white people who do not, of course, live in Harlem. Even the Negro members are apt, in the course of a conversation, to say something like, "Since I've been in New York . . ."

"You know, it seems like all of us are from some other part of the country," says a young member newly in from Connecticut.

The Black Muslims are segregationists, who preach a doctrine of separation from the "blue-eyed white devil" and who apparently originated the expression "whitey" for a white man, the Negro's comeback to the term "nigger," belatedly coined at a time when the North had come to consider that word a bit more shocking than an obscenity. The Muslims are militant and considered dangerous by many, but they are one of the groups in the Negro world which actually spread the message of moral discipline and self-help to people who are much more used to being dependent. The Muslims teach their members the economic facts of life and forbid them to drink or engage in sexual promiscuity. "They tell us not to spend all our money on food," a woman member says. "They make us dress like respectable people and act like respectable people and they tell us to save our money, so we can buy businesses and not have to depend on the white man." The Black Muslims' doctrine of self-help can take other forms. They have a very tough bodyguard unit, the Fruit of Islam, which was blamed last spring not only for beating up two men at a rally, but for holding back police who tried to get through the crowd to stop the beating.

The charlatans are apparent everywhere, but they seem most prominent in the black nationalist groups, where they have managed to achieve some standing among whites as Harlem leaders. Editors have given credence to men too ridiculous and not nearly funny enough to be written into Amos 'n' Andy scripts. Off camera, they go to the corner of Seventh Avenue and 125th Street ("I call it Harlem's Hyde Park," says Inspector Kruszewski), where they harange idlers with inflammatory speeches against the white man and in favor of their own philosophy, pass the hat until they collect five or six dollars, then leave quickly. Police say that following some of them will lead you to a crap game.

Few of the newer Harlem leaders have any notable followings. An exception is Jesse Gray, whose Community Council on Housing has grass roots support in the cause of fighting absentee and negligent landlords. Gray, with a left-wing background and fiery ideas, has been condemned on many grounds, but he does have a following.

Other leaders in Harlem, such as the Reverend Robert M. Kinloch, the Reverend Nelson C. Dukes, Sr., Edward Mills Davis, James Lawson, and sundry nationalists appear to be strongest on sound and fury, but their sound is loud and their fury can be communicated.

It is worth noting that Kinloch and Dukes squabbled

loudly and publicly early this year when Kinloch threw a few shabby pickets in front of a lunchroom on 125th Street, demanding "more black faces behind the counter" and Dukes appeared to negotiate a settlement between him and the employer. Kinloch screamed that Dukes was interfering in his demonstration. The Negro dishwasher in the lunchroom said he didn't want to wait on counters. The two Puerto Rican countermen, members of another minority but not dark enough to suit Kinloch, looked confused.

Communists are no longer a large group in Harlem, but the Communist influence is there in the Progressive Labor Movement, whose head, William Epton, describes himself as a follower of the Chinese Communists. The PLM is not large in membership, but it is a force in the community and is believed to have been a factor in the 1964 riots.

Nearly all sources agree that the man best equipped with the brains, leadership and following necessary to elevate the people of Harlem is the Reverend Adam Clayton Powell, member of Congress from Harlem and pastor of the 10,000-member Abyssinian Baptist Church, which was built by his father. The Reverend Adam Clayton Powell has solved any pangs of conscience about uniting church and state in his person by being an absentee pastor of his church, running its affairs from his home in Puerto Rico through assistant pastors. His appearances at the church are infrequent, but no one seems to care. Nor do they care about his record of attendance in the House of Representatives or his record for seeing the world on congressional funds.

There are people in Harlem who feel that terror plays a large part in its politics. If so, it has never attracted public notice, but, since politics is a rough-and-tumble business and Harlem is a rough-and-tumble place, this idea is not to be lightly dismissed. Probably very few people in Harlem—even the richest—feel completely safe. A Negro can seldom acquire any more importance than the white establishment or popularity among his own people gives him. A Harlem Negro whose own people turn against him and who is not supported by the white establishment is in bad shape, no matter how much power he may appear to have.

Whether terror is important in Harlem politics or not, demagoguery is. It is a basic rule of politics that it is easier to be elected by fighting *against* something or someone, rather than fighting *for* something or someone. In Harlem, to get elected, you must charge that your opponent is a lackey of the hated white man, and defend yourself against charges of being an "Uncle Tom." Campaign speeches, therefore, are not calculated to improve race relations. The fortunate campaigner must, after his election, demonstrate to his constituents that he does not take any guff from the white establishment. That doesn't improve race relations, either.

In fact, the only noticeable action taken in race relations for several months preceding the 1964 Harlem riots was inflammation. Negroes were subjected to a constant stream of stories in their own newspapers and the city dailies about their mistreatment. They were studied and restudied by psychologists, sociologists, magazine writers, and television crews. They were exhorted by civil rights zealots, black confidence men, and crackpot nationalists. All these students gushed pity on them. A few—usually an evangelist or a Muslim—suggested that a little self-help might improve their lot enormously and that it was time for Negroes, a century away from the white massa, to wean themselves from the eating, drinking, and breeding habits of the slave, develop a little responsibility, and start building the basic unit of Western civilization—the family.

National civil rights leaders, ever given to the catch phrase, spent the winter predicting "a long, hot summer." To the wild youngsters of Harlem who wear latchkeys around their necks because there is no one at home to let them into the tenement apartment when they return from school, this meant violence. To the men who lounge around Lenox Avenue, wondering how to get the price of a drink or how to squirm into a bed, it also meant violence.

Actually, the violence had started before the talk of the "long, hot summer."

The Harlem volcano had staged minor eruptions frequently since 1943. In 1949, the late Ben Davis, the Communist then representing Harlem in the City Council, decided to hold a torchlight parade on Lenox Avenue without a permit. When police tried to stop the parade, bricks and bottles flew. Six policemen were injured and six persons arrested before the fight ended.

On July 28 and 29, 1961, a thousand Negroes battled police in Harlem after a mob trying to force its way into the 28th Precinct had been dispersed. Newspapers, for some reason, described the action as a "near riot." There were broken windows and there was a little looting.

In June, 1963, with civil rights a hot issue, New York was braced for trouble in Harlem. It came on the seventeenth, when a policeman arrested an ice-cream vendor on the fringe of a rally at Harlem's "Hyde Park." The vendor protested, the crowd was angered, bottles and bricks flew, and the night became wild before a mounted police charge turned the tide. There were twenty-five persons arrested and police braced themselves for a repeat of 1943, but

Bayard Rustin's March on Washington took the energy out of the volcano.

The evil feeling against the white man cropped out next in October, when Julius Bulgach, seventy-one, who had been peddling fruit from a horse-drawn wagon since Harlem's fashionable days, was ordered to hand over his money. Mr. Bulgach had been through this sort of nonsense before, and his motto, often expressed, was, "Let 'em have the money." But this time, for reasons which will never be known, he demurred. He kept his $172, and lost his life. A knife flashed and the little man known affectionately to Negroes in the neighborhood as "Shorty" staggered to a stoop at 159 West 131st Street and curled up, remarking, "I am hurt." When the Reverend Martin Ling, of nearby St. Mark's Roman Catholic Church, offered him Extreme Unction, he said, "Father, I'm Jewish," and the priest said, "I'll pray for you anyway." A prowl car rushed him down the street to Harlem Hospital, but nothing could be done for him. It was just another Harlem murder —one among several—but it was widely talked about in Harlem, and more fuel for the fire.

At this time, David Watts, twenty-nine years old, blond, blue-eyed, and slender, was wandering around Harlem, Bible in hand, extending Christian love to his fellow man, regardless of skin color. David had arrived in New York from California in 1957, looked up the address of an Adventist church in the telephone book and shown up at the Advent Sabbath Church, 255 West 131st Street. The Reverend Thomas Hughes pointed out that he was the only white person in the congregation, but David said he'd stay. He impressed the people of Harlem as a saintly person. In March, 1964, a young Negro poked a knife into David, and no one was ever able to guess why. On April

37

1, the congregation held his funeral at another, larger church. It was attended by five hundred persons. Two women fainted. Many mourners wept throughout the services. Nineteen ministers and evangelists eulogized David in the course of the service, which lasted two hours and forty-three minutes in a sort of atonement for what the people considered an atrocity.

On April 11, 1964, Miss Eileen Johnston, twenty-eight, a welfare worker only recently arrived from Chicago, left Count Basie's Night Club, where she had spent an evening with a Negro co-worker. They were only a few steps from the door of the nightclub when two youths moved toward her and one of them said, "This one's mine." A knife flashed, sank into the young woman's back, and Miss Johnston fell dead.

Then, a social worker, on duty, was accosted in a tenement by an eighteen-year-old Negro with a knife, taken to the roof, and raped.

On April 17, a gang of youths passing a fruit stand at 128th Street and Lenox Avenue overturned it and began pelting each other with fruit. Police who got to the scene grabbed a couple of the slower boys, but the rest, plus some adults, came back to rescue them. Rocks, rubbish, and carbage-can lids flew, and sixteen cops finally managed to extricate their fellows and disperse the mob. They arrested five persons, including Daniel Hamm, eighteen, who later confessed to killing Miss Johnston, and Wallace Baker, nineteen. About thirty teen-agers came to the station to charge police brutality and were later joined by representatives of Malcolm X's dissident band of Black Muslims. It ended without further rioting.

Twelve days later, Mrs. Magit Sugar, a forty-seven-year-old Hungarian refugee, was working in the clothing store she and her husband, Frank, operated at 125th Street and Fifth Avenue. Six or eight youths entered the store and asked to be shown a suit. Mrs. Sugar was frightened by their arrogance and refused to serve them. One of the youths, later identified by police as Wallace Baker, pulled a double-edged dirk and stabbed her repeatedly. Her husband ran to help her and, in the shrieking tumult that ensued, suffered several stab wounds before he won possession of the knife and the gang fled. None of the commotion had attracted any help from the crowds passing outside. Police found a scene so gore-spattered that blood dripped from a display raincoat. Mrs. Sugar was dead and her husband critically wounded.

Baker and Hamm confessed to the murders. At this writing, their trials have not been completed and their guilt or innocence has not been established. A story appeared in the *New York Times* that the four hundred members of a youth organization called the "Blood Brothers" were being trained to kill whites. This was never corroborated, but police in the area insist there was something similar to that going on and that it ended with the two arrests.

All these events were transpiring against the background of school boycotts, rent strikes, the World's Fair stall-in, and the whole civil rights ferment. White people in Harlem could feel the tension rising, especialy policemen, the visible sign of white power, the men who enforce the rather erratic law and order in Harlem.

On a hot day in Harlem, the tenements and rooming houses become unbearable, and the occupants quite sensibly move outside. They are likely to remain there most of the night, the older people sitting on the stoops, drinking, playing cards, or singing, the children playing in the streets. The teen-agers and adults may head for the avenues and stand in huge, dark clusters or elbow through the crowds. Day or night, the cops like to keep the crowds down, and there are frequent instructions to "break it up" or "move along." These bring arguments.

There also are the water hydrants, an irresistible temptation to hot people who want to cool off. In May, June, and early July, the 28th Precinct had an average of more than forty complaints of open hydrants per shift in its .56-square-mile area. New York has to be thrifty about its water and police have to turn off the hydrants. This is a dangerous business in Harlem. It arouses resentment, which is often expressed by a brick thrown from the roof of a six-story building. For this reason, standing orders are that no policeman is to go alone to turn off a hydrant; there must be two men and both must wear steel helmets. Even so, policemen have been disabled at this job.

Police are *not* liked in Harlem. Negroes usually explain that it is because they are brutal and corrupt, to which police enter a vigorous dissent. Inspector Kruszewski gives a stock reason when he says the hatred is caused by the fact that police are the only visible sign of the white power structure and these victims of deprivation and discrimination tend to take out their frustrations on police. Another often-given and logical reason is that the Southern Negro comes to Harlem not necessarily in search of freedom, but expecting to find it there and determined to enjoy it. He resents any curb on his personal activities by policemen and it seems likely to many that he takes out on Northern policemen the angers he built up against Southern policemen but didn't dare to show. But even many Northern Negroes seem to have a latent hostility to policemen, often traceable to the times that ignorant or unthinking cops

40

gave them the "move on" or "what are you doing in this neighborhood, buddy" treatment. Few slum Negroes approach policemen in a calm state of mind, and the slightest disagreement with them is apt to lead to shouting which borders on the hysterical and which requires almost superhuman coolness on the part of the officer.

What may irritate police most is the reluctance of so many Negroes to help in preserving law and order in their own neighborhoods. A policeman arresting a law-breaker may receive interference from people who never saw the prisoner before he was under arrest and have no idea of what he has done. Detectives say it is difficult even to get wounded people to name their assailants unless the victim can be convinced he is going to die and therefore won't be able to avenge himself. Add to this the stream of lies and deceits directed toward the police, the bricks thrown from rooftops, sometimes at a policeman attempting to help a Negro who has collapsed on the sidewalk, and the disgusting crimes frequently committed, and you may begin to understand why the policeman's estimation of the Harlem Negro in general is not high.

But policemen work in Harlem without loud complaint. A policeman's work is dirty at its best and, even in Harlem, things seldom get so bad that they can't fight their way out of it. The speakers rail at 125th Street, the heat magnifies emotions, someone says, "Let's go to 123rd Street," and the mob starts its short, noisy walk down Seventh Avenue and turns into 123rd Street.

Half a block away, in the 28th Precinct, policemen grab their nightsticks and fall in out front, reminding themselves of the old departmental joke that the New York Police Department has never lost a precinct yet. Usually, the demonstration consists only of yelling and

41

singing, a little shoving, the placing of barricades across the street to keep the crowd back from the entrance, and a visit by a committee to express the crowd's grievances. Sometimes, there is some fighting.

"This is the only governmental office they have," says Inspector Kruszewski. "This is their version of city hall. If they're going to demonstrate against the government, they have to do it here."

It didn't occur to him or to the man he was talking to until much later that there are three welfare offices in Harlem which are visible, busy representatives of the government and they are *never* attacked.

But July, 1964, was different. In the streets, the people of Harlem were talking about a fifteen-year-old Negro boy named James Powell, who had been killed by a white policeman. A lieutenant. They said the boy had a knife. But you'd think a big man could take a knife away from a little boy like that without killing him, wouldn't you? Anyway, he shot him twice. Why'd he have to shoot twice? Only fifteen years old . . .

3

Saturday, July 18

At 2 P.M. on Saturday, July 18, 1964, the temperature
in New York was recorded as 92 degrees. That measure-
ment was taken in Central Park, the green oasis on Manhattan Island. Out on the cement that covers most of
the city, the temperature was much higher. Up in Harlem,
in the old brownstones and the tenements, the temperature must have been well over 100 degrees. Worse was
that there had been a whole series of days when the temperature in Central Park had risen to 80 degrees or more.
The heat had collected in the masonry of the buildings,
so that the Negroes there could almost bake in their beds.
They may not have been alone in their sufferings, but they
were suffering. There is a definite correlation between
heat and Negro riots. If that day had been a cool one,
there very likely would have been no riot. But it was a
sizzler.

In the afternoon, police were prominent at the Levy and
Delany Funeral Home, on Seventh Avenue at 132nd
Street. They had barricades nearby, in case any trouble

should develop, but there was no difficulty with the 250 persons who filed past young Powell's casket. His mother collapsed at the funeral home, crying, "They killed my baby! They murdered my baby. That's all it was. Murder."

Police also stood by at a demonstration at Second Avenue and 76th Street, where residents of the area around the Wagner School were demonstrating to call attention to the rising crime rate.

Both the wake and the demonstration passed without incident, and those who worry about such things breathed more easily. The next hurdle for peace and order was a CORE rally, which had been scheduled by several chapters some time previously to protest the disappearance of three civil rights workers in Mississippi. The CORE leaders had changed the object of protest to "police brutality" in the Powell shooting. This struck police and newspaper editors as potentially explosive, so the meeting was well attended by cops and reporters. But it seemed a rather routine rally.

There was no loudspeaker system, so only a few of the passersby and loungers at the corner gathered to listen when a pretty seventeen-year-old Negro girl named Judith Howell, a Bronx high-school student and a member of the Bronx chapter of CORE, climbed on a rickety blue café chair and started a denunciation and accusation of Lieutenant Gilligan.

Miss Howell wore a boy's button-down shirt, a skirt, and loafers without socks. Her first words were:

"I'm mad. I'm so damn' mad tonight. I'm not much older than that boy and I'm scared of every cop out here."

The crowd murmured its approval and someone shouted, "That's the way to go, little girl."

The teen-ager launched into a tirade against Lieutenant Gilligan. "We got a civil rights bill and along with the bill we got Barry Goldwater and a dead black boy," she shouted. "This shooting of James Powell was murder!"

When Miss Howell stepped down for other speakers, the cry was for action.

"It is time to let 'the man' (a Negro term for the white man) know that if he does something to us we are going to do something back," shouted Chris Sprowal, chairman of the Downtown chapter of CORE. "If you say, 'You kick me once, I'm going to kick you twice,' we might get some respect."

But Mr. Sprowal was interrupted by Miss Howell, now a member of the audience, when he referred to the plea by the wife of Herb Callender, Bronx CORE chairman, for a peaceful protest demonstration. (Callender had been sent to Bellevue for a mental examination. He was arrested after trying a citizen's arrest on Mayor Robert Wagner.)

"If I was Herb Callender's wife, I'd have said, 'Let's go down to that precinct and take it apart brick by brick,'" shouted Miss Howell.

The next speaker was Charles Saunders of South Jamaica CORE, who charged that "forty-five percent of the cops in New York are neurotic murderers."

The CORE rally ended with the crowd excited, but not unruly. The reporters who were present took the emotional temperature and decided they would be more valuable to their newspapers elsewhere. Nearly all left. One of the few exceptions was Paul L. Montgomery, assistant religious editor of the *New York Times*, who was on one of those "on your way home" assignments that reporters know so well. The regular civil rights reporters had dismissed this rally as not likely to produce anything newsworthy and the city desk had suggested that since Montgomery lived more or less in the direction of Harlem, he might cover it, then go home. He became engrossed in the street drama and stayed after most other reporters went about their business, a decision which he was to regret periodically during the hours to come, but which made him one of the leading authorities on the beginning of the Harlem riot.

The CORE speakers were followed by the Reverend Nelson C. Dukes, of the Fountain Springs Baptist Church, who spent twenty minutes telling the crowd it was time to stop talking. He urged that the crowd march on the police station, but, says Deputy Chief Thomas V. Pendergast, he did not say which station. Dukes was followed by Edward Mills Davis, a black nationalist, who urged action, and then by James Lawson.

Now, the crowd was getting more excited and when Dukes shouted from the sidewalk, "Let's go to the station," they started. Inspector Pendergast estimates that 250 persons joined the march south on Seventh Avenue two short blocks, then into 123rd Street. At the 28th Precinct, patrolmen at the door locked arms to hold the crowd out, while other men in the station grabbed their equipment and ran to help. At the urging of the police, the crowd retreated to the sidewalk and selected a committee to enter and state their grievance.

The committee, consisting of Dukes, Charles Russell of the East River CORE, and Charles Taylor and Newton Sewell, both identified by police as black nationalists, entered the station and demanded of Inspector Pendergast that Lieutenant Gilligan be suspended. Inspector Pendergast pointed out that the shooting was being investigated by both the district attorney and Police Commissioner Michael J. Murphy, and the committee left.

So far, it was not an unusual demonstration for a Harlem precinct. Outside, Inspector Pendergast gave Dukes and Russell his bullhorn so they could address the crowd, but the crowd would not listen. Inspector Pendergast ordered them to the sidewalk across the street from the precinct, and his men pushed them back, but now the crowd was definitely ugly.

Young men and women pushed their faces up close to those of the patrolmen and chanted, "Murder, murder, murder." An impromptu song began; to the tune of the civil rights song, "We Shall Not Be Moved," the crowd sang "Murphy is a bastard, he must be removed." From the tops of the tenements, a few bottles came flying down and crashed in the street. Montgomery ducked to the stoop of a tenement next to the police station, where he stood with a middle-aged Negro woman, both of them watching the scene with some interest.

Policemen donned steel air-raid-warden-type helmets and moved into the tenements, went up the stairs, and took over the roofs, ending the aerial bombardment. Barricades were called for and, as police removed them from the truck and put them into position, a scuffle broke out, and about twenty-five people, including some policemen, fell to the pavement.

CORE charged later that Inspector Pendergast shouted through his bullhorn at this point: "Lock those niggers up!"

Inspector Pendergast denied the racial slur, and few who know him would doubt him. He was backed by Montgomery, who says the cry was: "Lock them up."

CORE members promptly dropped into their characteristic position for arrest—arms over the heads and knees doubled up against the chest. They were carried into the stationhouse. Others who did not adopt the passive position were grabbed, usually by more than one policeman, and pulled swiftly into the stationhouse. Montgomery considered these latter as rough arrests, with each policeman tending to pull in a different direction on the same prisoner, but no clubs were used. A total of fourteen were plucked out of the crowd and put into cells in a very short time.

The shouting in the crowd increased, and bottles and rubbish began to rain into the police ranks. A bottle hit Patrolman Michael Doris in the face and he fell, the first policeman injured.

Dukes, who had been wearing a bewildered expression, said, "If I'd known this was going to happen, I wouldn't have said anything." He disappeared.

Inspector Pendergast had had enough. "This has become a disorderly gathering," he said through the bullhorn. "I am instructing the police to clear the street."

Patrolmen were pouring out of the stationhouse now and they began to move the crowd toward the two avenues at the end of the block. "Everybody off the block or on your stoop," they told the crowd, which retreated before them, still shouting but not resisting. Montgomery saw no clubs used. About half the crowd was herded down to Eighth Avenue at the western end of the block, where it melted away after barricades were put up and police manned them. The other half was herded to Seventh Avenue, where it remained just outside the barricades.

Two blocks up Seventh Avenue, at 125th Street, Lawson's group was still holding one of its Saturday night rallies. Most of his audience immediately adjourned to the barricades. The rumor which reached Lawson was that a prisoner had been beaten. He and Edward Mills Davis proceeded indignantly to the station, where they demanded an investigation. The lieutenant on duty produced the prisoner, who denied the rumors. "They may have been a little rough when they arrested me," he said, "but they haven't bothered me in here." The committee of two went back to Seventh Avenue.

There the crowd had swelled to immense size. By 10 P.M. there were about a thousand people milling in the intersection, by Inspector Pendergast's estimate. Police were being thoroughly vilified. Voice after voice after voice hurled the lower-class Negro's favorite epithet in adjectival form: "mother ——— whiteys." Voices raised chants against "police brutality," and voices branded them murderers.

The feeling and the crowds were spreading. A white compact car coming up Lenox Avenue with a white couple in it was surrounded by Negroes who pounded on the top and sides. One Negro stepped to the front of the car, drew back a bottle, and smashed a headlight with it. The driver inched the car forward until he was free of the crowd and then zoomed away, the little car careening from side to side, indicating his fright.

The Harlem rooftop is the policeman's enemy. There is easy access to the roof of any tenement. Deputy Chief Inspector Harry Taylor, commander of Manhattan North area, had attempted to lessen the danger during the spring by ordering his men to inspect the rooftops and clear them of any rubbish which might be heaved at them, but it was a hopeless task. The buildings are old, the mortar is crumbling, and bricks are easily picked loose. Between each building is a parapet, with a tile covering that can almost always be pulled off to uncover a brick-heaver's armory. The tiles themselves are no mean weapons when dropped five or six stories.

An officer with a bullhorn appeared at the intersection and shouted through it: "Go home, go home." Back from the crowd came the voice of Harlem: "We are home, Baby."

The crowd was picking up emotion, feeding it on rumors, obscenities, and reports of supposed eyewitnesses to the arrests in front of the precinct. "They beat those kids," was the word passed around and around the intersection.

Now, the bricks began to come from the rooftops, but reinforcements had arrived. The Tactical Patrol Force, every member of it under thirty years of age, at least six feet tall, trained in judo and riot control, and full of esprit de corps, was on the scene. Chief Taylor also was on the scene and had decided it was time to act.

The TPF was ordered to clear the madhouse intersection. Working in squad-sized flying wedges, a sergeant at the point and all the men waving their clubs and yelling "Charge!" they plowed through the crowd, breaking it into small segments, then driving the segments away from the intersection.

And then hell broke loose in Harlem.

As nearly as anyone can reconstruct it, the mob that was sent south on Seventh Avenue pulled fire alarms, set fire to rubbish baskets, and chased any whites they met, beating some. Fire engines answering the false alarms added to the tumult of the night.

But it was the part of the crowd that went north from 123rd Street that was most vicious. The next day—in fact, later that night—this mob could be traced by its damage. It went up to 125th Street, turned right to Lenox Avenue, and then turned north again, leaving a trail of broken windows and looted stores clear to 135th Street. Part of it turned left at 125th Street and went to Eighth Avenue.

For the most part, the merchants had anticipated them. At the first sign of trouble, most Harlem store-owners had put up the folding gates which guard their windows at night, locked their stores, and left Harlem for their homes.

But the mob hooked chains to the folding gates, then pulled them off the windows with automotive power. Some of the people brought crowbars to pry the gates loose. Windows shattered and whole inventories disappeared into the streets.

Now, special measures were being taken. Traffic was being blocked on most of the avenues into Harlem. Buses were being rerouted to avoid Harlem, and Transit Authority policemen were being sent to the subway stations to secure them against the mobs.

Then, a crowd leaving the IND subway at St. Nicholas Avenue and 125th Street moved west peaceably until it met another peaceable crowd leaving the Apollo Theater near Eighth Avenue. Refugees from the action at the precinct were moving around the intersection, shouting garbled tales of what had happened there. The crowd was now very large and was growing more excited. A window shattered.

Montgomery had followed the police as they chased the crowd north on Seventh Avenue, but he stopped at the Theresa Hotel, listening to the sound of breaking glass on 125th Street. At 10:30 P.M., a Molotov cocktail, the instrument used so effectively during World War II by Russian partisans to set fire to Nazi tanks, flew through the air in front of the hotel. It didn't look very impressive —a bottle full of liquid with a tongue of flame coming from a piece of cloth stuffed in its mouth. But it hit beside

51

a police car, smashed, and a pool of fire leaped in the street. The policemen in the car sprang out, and Patrolman Frank Strazza stepped into the pool, burning his leg severely. The other policemen drew their guns and began to fire into the air. It was the first gunfire of the night.

In the city room of the *Herald Tribune,* a reporter answered the telephone, and a Negro man asked him how he could contact Governor Rockefeller. The reporter said he didn't know and asked what the trouble was, wondering idly about the popping noises audible in the background as the other man talked. "That Goldwater stuff has started," the Negro said. "They're shooting at people up here in Harlem. The police are chasing the people here at Eighth Avenue and 125th Street and shooting at them."

It dawned on the reporter that the popping noise was gunfire—a lot of it.

"Have they killed any of them?" he asked.

"No, they're shooting in the air," the man said. "The crowd runs when they shoot, then, when they stop, the crowd comes back again."

The press corps went back to Harlem.

The shots in the air soon had been adopted as a tactic and were in use at Eighth Avenue. They proved the only defense against the missiles from the rooftops, since they drove back even the most fanatic bombers, and they were also effective in moving the crowds. Police Commissioner Murphy says the order to fire in the air was given by the field commanders and that he approved it when he arrived on the scene.

Reporters who came hurrying to Harlem found a warlike atmosphere at the precinct, with helmeted patrolmen guarding the barricades at the end of the block, more helmeted patrolmen checking identification of everyone who attempted to enter the station, scores of reinforcements being briefed before they marched out to battle, cars bringing in prisoners, who often were bruised and bleeding and, with it all, senior officers attempting to find civic leaders who might be able to restore calm in the area. Shortly after this, policemen were instructed not to bring prisoners to the 28th Precinct, but to take them to other stationhouses, less crowded and less likely to draw mobs bent on freeing the prisoners.

When reporters moved down to Seventh Avenue, they found things even more warlike. They met a huge hostility in the population. The *Herald Tribune*'s Joseph Endler moved through a crowd in which a man kept saying, "We oughtta kill that whitey." He made it to a bar, found a telephone, and called in his story as an intoxicated woman in a nearby booth rocked back and forth and chanted, "Don't kill our babies. Don't kill our colored babies."

Actually, there seemed to be a lull at that time. At midnight, Montgomery, still on Seventh Avenue, heard a fantastic volley of shots from Lenox and 125th and ran a block to find police breaking up a huge crowd there. After that, no one could keep track of the incidents. Police were receiving calls to help beleaguered policemen at fifteen-second intervals. Strings of squad cars were racing through the streets, their red lights flashing, in answer to the calls. Gunfire was almost continuous in Harlem, breaking out first in one place, then a couple of blocks away, then again a couple of blocks in another direction. But the fall of bricks and bottles from roofs and windows also was almost continuous, and the streets were soon deep with broken glass, so that patrol cars were put out of action with flat tires. There is a suspicion that more than

53

one freshly emptied gin bottle was hurled to the street more as a handy means of disposal than as a weapon, but there also is evidence that many normally law-abiding people caught the spirit, ran to their rooftops, and donated a brick to the Police Department.

When Montgomery got to Lenox, he found that some twenty police cars had gone to the intersection and had been followed by a crowd nearly as large as the one police were trying to disperse. A ring of policemen stood in the middle of the street, while hundreds of Negroes stood on each corner, many of them throwing bottles. Police gathered themselves and charged into the crowds, firing into the air and swinging their clubs for effect. The police cars began a shuttle service for prisoners taken at the intersection.

The action was being repeated at each intersection north from Lenox. Another *Times* reporter, Francis X. Clines, one of those sent to reinforce Montgomery, decided to take a look at events above 125th Street.

Just north of the intersection, he found two patrolmen crouching behind their squad car, firing their pistols occasionally. "Are we shooting *at* them?" he heard one policeman ask the other.

Clines did not get beyond 126th Street. At that point, a young teen-ager hit him on the head with a two by four, then, as he fell, kicked him and called him vile names. Another Negro youth moved in, however, drove off Clines's assailant and helped him to a squad car. "Tell the people what's going on up here," he told the reporter.

Clines, the first reporter to be injured in the riots, sat in the car until his head cleared, puzzling over the remark. His savior was by no means the last person to tell a reporter to get the news out. As nearly as reporters could interpret the remarks, those who made them felt that

Negroes were being attacked by the police in a sort of pogrom. The obvious fact that police—and even unarmed reporters—were being attacked did not impress them.

Unlike soldiers, policemen do not carry large stocks of ammunition, so there came a point during this wild night when many of the men breaking up crowds were running out bullets. A special ordnance truck was improvised, loaded with boxes of .38-caliber ammunition, guarded by one policeman armed with a shotgun and another armed with a machine gun, and sent from the police pistol range in the Bronx to Harlem, where the ammunition was distributed.

Montgomery had made the trip up to 135th Street, thanks to the fact that he had been a track man in high school ten years before. He found much the same situation there as at 125th and then ran back, past crowds of Negroes, some of whom turned from looting stores to stare at him in wonder. At 125th, police still held the intersection, but the crowds still pressed them. Montgomery stood near the policemen, with a prowl car between him and the crowd on the west side of Lenox. Then, without any warning, the police shifted to the west side of the intersection to break up the crowd there, and the car pulled away, leaving the reporter suddenly exposed.

A large young Negro eyed Montgomery for a moment, then grabbed the tall slender white man and threw him up against a store front. "Whatcha doin' up in Harlem, White Britches?" he asked. He pushed Montgomery again and again into a grating which guarded the broken windows of the store. A crowd was gathering around. Montgomery, being pushed again, saw a bottle in someone's hand and a shard of broken window beside his face. He doesn't remember the next few seconds, but he found himself running toward Seventh Avenue, faster than he had ever run in a track meet, so fast his feet seemed not to touch the ground. When he reached the police line at Seventh Avenue, he turned to face his pursuers, but found they had stopped halfway back on the block and were gaping at the speedster who outran them.

When the crowd lost interest in him, Montgomery ran back to Lenox and into the ring of policemen. Shooting in the air and clubbings no longer made any impression on him. Men with bloody heads were commonplace in the crowd. Epithets which once had seemed blood-curdling to him now were part of the conversation.

A sleek, large, middle-aged man in Bermuda shorts, knee-length socks, jacket, and Madras tie sidled up to the barricade behind which Montgomery and Clines were sheltered and eyed the press badges pinned to their coats. "These are not the real people of Harlem," he said, gravely. "These are not the people who make Harlem great. Tell your readers that there is a good element in Harlem, that most of the people of Harlem are respectable and law-abiding." Dutifully, the two reporters made notes, and he went away.

A few minutes later, a screaming mob charged at the police and the two reporters were startled to see their portly instructor in the rear of it, his bare knees pumping and his fist waving in the air as he screamed, "Kill the mother————whiteys!"

"Some of the good people just got caught up in it, I guess," Montgomery says.

Some good people, both Negro and white, were getting caught up in the riot in a very bad way. Many Negroes were unaware, in spite of the sirens and gunfire, of the action in Harlem. They wandered out of side streets or subway entrances, found themselves in a crowd of running, screaming people, stood bewildered, and then found the pursuing policemen on them, swinging the heavy clubs.

Some Harlemites were victims of their own naïveté. In the steaming heat, nearly all the tenement dwellers had gone to the streets, and many of them, hearing of the excitement, went to look at it in the belief that rioting was a spectator sport. Police, unable to distinguish a rioter from a spectator, knowing only that crowds had to be broken up, were as tough with them as with the hostile population. The result was injuries to spectators and, in many cases, conversion of spectators into players.

At one point, policemen found a dark, silent cluster of men gathered under a light in a playground. The men had a conspiratorial appearance, and police approached them quietly, ready for anything. They surrounded a group of Negroes who regularly played Spanish checkers through the night in the park and who had no intention of giving up their game just because some nuts were staging a riot. They were willing to continue the game in jail, if necessary. The police fell back, grinning, under a barrage of indignant curses.

Whites who drove into Harlem found their cars surrounded and violence threatening them. The news of the riot had been late getting out and had not spread thoroughly through New York. Motel-owner Jack Lambert, twenty-nine, and a friend, Carolyn Fawcett, twenty-four, somehow wandered into Harlem at 3:30 A.M. in a convertible and stopped for a light at 127th Street and Lenox Avenue. A mob surounded the car and started hurling rocks at it. Lambert tried to put up the top and told his companion to lie down for protection, but before she could, the mob began beating the couple with boards and rocks. Before the TPF could battle its way to the convertible, Miss Fawcett had suffered head cuts, and Lambert had a dislocated shoulder.

The *Herald Tribune* was reinforcing its Harlem crew, also. Bill Whitworth, twenty-seven years old, fair of skin and hair and with a voice which serves notice of his Arkansas origin, was dispatched from home to Harlem. Whitworth is a jazz buff and had been in the habit of going to Harlem for entertainment. "The jazz is as good as it is downtown and there's no cover or mimimum," he says. "But I stopped going there after Eileen Johnston was killed. Nobody had bothered me, but I lost my confidence."

Routed from bed and still sleepy, he didn't regain any of his confidence on the subway. The Lenox Avenue IRT line drops most of its white passengers when the Columbia University crowd switches to the local at 96th Street. Whitworth was the only white person left on the train after that. He pinned his press badge to his coat and sat quietly until the train stopped at 125th Street. At 3 A.M., Transit Authority policemen were on the platform, refusing to let passengers off, but they yielded to his press card, telling him he was crazy to want to get off there. Whitworth was inclined to agree with them, but duty called. He poked his head cautiously from the entrance, saw a crowd but no action, and came up on the sidewalk. Instantly, he was surrounded by Negroes, who asked, "What are you doin' in Harlem, whitey?"

"My office sent me," Whitworth answered.

"Man, get out of here. This ain't no place for a white man tonight. What kind of office do you work for?"

"A newspaper. And I can't get out of here; I've got to work for a living."

He had said the right thing. The crowd adopted him and

when, a little later, Negroes made threats to him, his friends in the crowd told them to get lost. "He's just earnin' his bread," one man said.

However, he had been very fortunate to land in friendly hands. A few minutes later, bottles flew and police charged the crowd. Whitworth went out into the street and a policeman ordered him to the curb. When he went to the curb, another policeman told him to get in the middle of the street or he might get shot. He was shocked; until that time, he had thought the police were shooting blanks.

"I moved back and forth until dawn," he said. "I never saw such things."

Often, he was with the Negro spectators and he found them highly partisan, convinced that the policemen were the aggressors, in spite of the bricks, bottles, rubbish cans, and Molotov cocktails which flew around the intersection.

"They want to kill all of us," he heard an old woman say. "They want to shoot all the black people." A man agreed. "They wouldn't do all this gunslinging and clubbing on 42nd Street," he said.

About 3 A.M., Montgomery, wandering north from 125th and Lenox, had seen a large crowd at 127th Street and had turned into 126th to avoid it. As he walked along the quiet street, a woman came out of a brownstone and said, "Are you the man from NBC?" She had called NBC to report that a man had been killed on her roof. Police had shot him as he heaved bricks at them, she said. Montgomery questioned her long enough to make certain from her description that the man was dead, then turned to go to a telephone. Out of the darkness, a blue-clad figure loomed, and Montgomery relaxed when he saw it was a white policeman. "Are you going down to

Lenox?" the policeman asked. Montgomery said he was. "Do you mind if I walk with you?" the policeman asked. Montgomery said no and they walked in silence to the intersection, where the reporter turned south and the policeman turned north. He was one of the most puzzling figures of the riots, since he was the only foot patrolman seen who was not under command.

A man had been killed. Police had found him on the roof after a group of TPF men had fired in the air to drive brick-heavers back from the edge of the roof. They asked who did it and a patrolman raised his hand. The dead man was an ex-convict with a record of ten arrests, the police said, when they finally announced the slaying at a press conference four hours later.

Montgomery had made his way back to 123rd Street and Seventh Avenue, where police were still manning the barricades. With the avenues blocked north and south, there was no civilian traffic, and everyone was surprised to see a newspaper delivery truck come speeding up Seventh Avenue. The reporters were pleased. "There's a driver with guts," they told each other. "He means to see that those papers get through."

The truck screeched to a stop at the barricade and seven Negro teen-agers jumped from the back and fled. The driver jumped from the front, bleeding from the head and almost raving with anger. "Catch 'em!" he yelled. "Catch 'em and let me have just five minutes with 'em!" They had jumped into his truck when he stopped for a traffic light, he said, and had been beating him as he roared up Seventh Avenue for help.

About 4 A.M., a figure in bloody sailor's whites stumbled up to the same barricade. He said he had gotten lost on the subway, had gotten off the train and had been set upon by a gang of Negro teen-agers. "I told them I'm just a sailor from California who got lost, but they kept beating me," he said.

It was at the hospitals that the effect of the riot could best be seen that night. The path leading to the emergency entrance of Harlem Hospital was sprinkled with blood. Harlem and Sydenham hospitals were crowded with bleeding people, but one administrator said it was no more than triple the usual Saturday night business. Nevertheless, there were enough gunshot wounds and cuts to keep the surgeries busy, and there were many heads to be sewn up. Most patients said they had been minding their own business when they were shot or clubbed, although one man admitted he had thrown a brick at a policeman before he was clubbed. He said the policeman had called him a nigger.

Harlem Hospital's final count was seventy-five persons treated for riot injuries. Sydenham said it treated thirty. Knickerbocker Hospital said it had only four patients from the riot.

Louis Smith, a CORE field secretary who said he was just back from Mississippi, was at Harlem Hospital that night and was upset by what he saw. "This is worse than anything I ever saw in Mississippi," he said.

Police Commissioner Murphy arrived at the 28th Precinct about 4:30 A.M. and began meeting with what leadership Harlem could muster on a Saturday night— Madison Jones, executive director of the City Commission on Human Rights, Criminal Court Judge Kenneth M. Phipps, and James Lawson, the last suddenly elevated to importance. The group decided that Commissioner Murphy should write a letter to the people of Harlem and that it should be passed on through the churches and through sound trucks on the streets.

The rioting was dying a little and auto traffic already

was beginning to move on Lenox, most of it Negroes looking at the damaged stores. When dawn broke about 5 A.M., the sun illuminated a ghastly scene of broken windows; ransacked stores; streets littered with broken glass, rubbish, and empty cartridges; crowds of sullen Negroes; and tired policemen, semimilitary in their helmets. Most startling were the gates which merchants had put across their windows the night before and which now snaked crazily across the sidewalks amid the litter on Lenox, 125th, Seventh, and Eighth.

The crowd built up again on Lenox as men and women exhorted it. "Let's burn down the precincts and get all these bastards out of here," a woman shouted. By 7 A.M., tired policemen, slumped in doorways, were rousing themselves to charge into the crowd again. Then, at 8 o'clock, more police arrived and cleared the intersection.

Meanwhile, there had been a press conference and Police Commissioner Murphy had given the statistics for the night: 1 dead, 12 policemen and 19 civilians injured, 30 persons arrested, 22 business places looted.

The figures on injured policemen were exact, because policemen must report every scratch they receive.

But hospital records and the observations of reporters showed that the estimate of civilian injuries was much too low, hardly more than the seven reported gunshot wounds resulting from ricocheting bullets and potshots at looters. About 110 persons had considered their injuries serious enough for hospital attention. Many others had bandaged their own cuts and nursed their own bruises.

But a long, hot Saturday night was over and there was hope that Sunday might be better.

4

Sunday, July 19

Just as a modern American city more swiftly and surely
punishes litterbugs than murderers, so does it more efficiently clean its streets than keep order among its citizens.
Within a short time, city workers had swept 125th Street
clean of glass, debris, and garbage and were turning their
attention to the avenues. A middle-aged Negro woman,
clean, starched, and frilled, turned into Harlem's main
stem on her way to church services. She stopped in surprise at the sight of the helmeted policemen lining both
sides of 125th Street like parking meters.

"What's happening?" she asked. "Is the President in
town?"

President Johnson was not in town, although his
thoughts undoubtedly were. Also not in town was Mayor
Robert Wagner. He was on the island of Majorca, Spain.
An aide said he was keeping in close touch with the
situation and did not feel it was necessary for him to
return. The aide added that Mayor Wagner planned to
fly to Geneva, Switzerland, after attending a ceremony
in his honor in Majorca.

Left in control of the tense situation were Council President Paul R. Screvane and Police Commissioner Murphy.

The woman on her way to church was not alone in her surprise that things had been happening during the night. Apparently, many Harlemites slept through the bedlam. The morning newspapers, radio newscasts, and their own shocked observations brought them up to date quickly, and emotion seemed to well in them.

In some—probably most, because Harlemites are as conscious as the rest of us that only law and order separates humans from the jungle—the emotion was fear and disgust at the mob actions, but many automatically blamed police. There are a lot of cop-haters in Harlem, and people who had been caught in the crowds the night before or who had hung out of a tenement window to watch the action were quick to pass on their versions of what had happened. Their stories seldom agreed with the stories of police and reporters.

At his meeting with the civic leaders who could be mustered during the night, Commissioner Murphy had prepared a statement of the situation and, in churches throughout the community, ministers were reading:

To the members of the Harlem community:
In order to stop rumors that are being spread through the community, I want to tell you about what has been done and is being done about the unfortunate shooting of a Negro boy by Lieutenant Gilligan of this police department.

When this happened, I ordered the civilian complaint review board to step in at once. Extra investigators were assigned to get all the witnesses and obtain the truth, which is what we all want.

Also, the district attorney is making a separate investigation to give evidence to the grand jury to see if there should be a criminal trial. All possible speed will be made. Let us be fair and not make a judgment until all of the facts are in and all the witnesses are heard. If you know of any witnesses, have them come forward to police headquarters or to the district attorney's office and give evidence.

I have met with some of the prominent people of your community and we all join in appealing for calm, lawful action by our people.

Let us show that the community does not approve of violence.

Some persons have used this unfortunate incident as an excuse for looting and for vicious unprovoked attacks against police. These crimes have been met by swift and necessary police action. In our estimation, this is a crime problem and not a social problem.

During the night, one man was killed by the police as he threw bricks from a roof at passing motorists and pedestrians and refused to cease when warned to do so.

Another man was shot while looting a store and he is in Harlem Hospital.

Two persons have been hit by ricocheting bullets and are not serious. In addition, 16 civilians were injured and 32 arrests made. Six patrolmen were injured during this disturbance. Let us stop these disorders and restore order in our community.

Deputy Commissioner Walter Arm, director of community relations for the department, went around to the churches passing out the statement and was disturbed by what he saw.

"I never met such hatred," he said later. "And these were the respectable church-going people. I couldn't understand it."

The church-going community of Harlem may have resented his implied reproach to them. More than one Negro minister was quick to point out that the element that carries on riots is not the element that attends church on Sundays, and that had there been rioting in a white community, no one would have attempted to try and reach the mob at church services.

There obviously was going to be another bad night, although the worst was over. Commissioner Murphy later described Saturday night as the worst of the six riot nights which afflicted New York City.

"It was the problem of trying to get the men in and also wondering where it would break out next—South Jamaica, the South Bronx, or Bedford-Stuyvesant," he said. By Sunday morning, he had the men in.

The New York Police Department several years ago decided it was best never to say how many policemen were sent to such a situation. Reporters on the scene Sunday guessed there were at least 500. A later suggestion to Commissioner Murphy that his 26,000-man department could get 500 policemen to any given point within an hour brought the comment that, "We can do a lot better than that." It is likely that reporters' estimates of police manpower in Harlem were only half high enough.

Harlem's merchants came in from their homes in the suburbs, shook their heads at the condition of their property and started the cleanup job. Sam Zaben, owner of Paul's Supermarket at 126th Street and Lenox Avenue, waded through ankle-deep debris, surveying the damage. "I've been in Harlem twenty-seven years and I've never had a cross word with my customers," he said. "This wasn't anything personal." He might have gotten an argument on that point, even from those of his customers not involved in the rioting. Shopkeepers, especially in slums, are not usually objects of neighborhood affection.

Rioters had wrecked three of four grocery stores in the block between 126th and 127th Streets on Lenox. A clerk in one store said groceries had been left in the store, but

66

all the beer and cigarettes and about $2,000 in cash were missing. A clerk in the store that was untouched reasoned that it had escaped because it remained open all night. "Looters won't come in when you're open," he said.

Considerable fear was generated by the gaping, glassless window of a pawn shop which formerly had displayed rifles and shotguns. The missing weapons seemed to indicate that the looters now were well armed, but detectives explained that they themselves had taken the guns into protective custody shortly after the window was broken.

That incident underlined the uneasiness which pervaded the upper echelon of the riot fighters. It had not been long since Malcolm X, the dissident Muslim, had suggested that Negroes form rifle clubs which would be ready to fight for their rights. Now, from Cairo, Egypt, where he was watching the African summit crisis, Malcolm X announced, "There are probably more armed Negroes in Harlem than in any other spot on earth." He added, "If the people who are armed get involved in this, you can bet they'll really have something on their hands."

Screvane, with the thankless job of being acting mayor under such circumstances, issued a plea for calm and an eloquent argument for law and order.

"This most marvelous city in the world could be a shambles almost overnight without law and order," he said. "Our civic survival depends upon the rule of law, as enforced by the police and the courts. But law and order is not the business just of the police and courts. It is the business of every group of citizens, because it is the basis of survival and nowhere more so than in New York City. Those with even the least stake in our society have a stake in law and order. Let no one deliberately strike a hole in the dike of peace and order which protects us all."

Many Negro spokesmen just couldn't see it that way. Dr. Kenneth Clark, psychology teacher at City College and a director of HARYOU, was writing a lengthy and almost logical analysis of the riot for the *Herald Tribune.*

He quoted statistics from the HARYOU report to show that Harlem is afflicted with high rates of homicide, drug addiction, juvenile delinquency, veneral disease, and poverty; he pointed out that the victims of Negro crimes usually are Negroes and accused police and the courts of ignoring such crimes. Clark said Negro youth in both New York City and Jackson, Mississippi, see police and law enforcement officers "as adversaries who are as zealous in seeking to maintain the racial status quo as the most ardent segregationists."

"This is a most dangerous situation," he wrote, "which is supported by realities and will not be resolved by campaign rhetoric emphasizing a onesided approach to the problem of [apparently quoting Sen. Barry Goldwater] 'the growing menace of public safety, to life, limb and property, in homes, churches, playgrounds and places of business, particularly in our great cities, is the mounting concern of every responsible citizen.'

"This type of cynical political opportunism can only add to the explosiveness of an already difficult and complex social problem. It will incite the passions and hatreds of already unstable and prejudiced citizens and police officers."

Clark maintained that the burning of Negro churches in the South is violence in our streets, the killing of Negroes in the South is violence in our land, and the inability of the government to protect civil rights workers is anarchy.

Then, he judged the Powell-Gilligan case.

"Each time a police officer shoots and kills a Negro teen-ager, that is urban crime," he wrote.

"In a 'struggle' between a 15-year-old allegedly armed with a knife and an adult policeman armed with a gun, was it necessary or imperative that the 15-year-old be shot and killed by the policeman? And how was this possible?

"Would the answers to these and related questions reveal that the life of a Negro is as meaningless to some of the police in New York City as it is to the sheriffs of rural Mississippi?"

At noon, Dr. Clark's defense had not appeared, but it was becoming obvious that such logic prevailed in Harlem, and it was equally obvious that the emotion which causes rioting was not spent. Policemen lining the streets were receiving a steady stream of invective from the crowds.

A woman glared at a Negro policeman and yelled, "If you were my husband, I'd beat you to death."

A high-ranking police officer noted one youth spouting obscenities at a patrolman, who was beginning to smoulder. "I'll come back at 9:30," the youth said. "Watch out, then." "You do that," said the patrolman evenly. "You come back right on the dot, because I'll be here waiting for you." He raised his club meaningfully and the youth swaggered away.

It occurred to the police official then that it would be a very good idea to change the men on riot duty in Harlem. "After a while, it began to get to them," he explained. "Human beings can only take so much of that stuff."

Herald Tribune columnist Jimmy Breslin, driving

through Harlem, found his car blocked by a fire engine on a slum side street. A teen-ager swaggered up to the car and made references to sinking a knife in "your fat, white belly," oblivious of a fireman who stood behind him, holding an ax. Empty as the threat might have been, it was indicative of the feelings.

The teen-agers of Harlem were obviously planning to get into the act and police were making command decisions about riot-control tactics. Mounted police, usually very effective in riot control, were ruled out of Harlem as too vulnerable to rooftop bombings and Molotov cocktails. Tear gas also was ruled out because a grenade thrown in the street would not stop rooftop activity and would inevitably send gas into the tenements to cause suffering among nonrioters, including children. Police will not say why fire hoses were vetoed, but it is known that the International Association of Firefighters is on record against use of firemen to control mobs.

The problem of the police was that they had to fight on two levels: street and rooftop. The problem was never really solved. Helicopters were brought in to watch the roofs and report activity there, but otherwise the previous night's tactics remained in use.

In early afternoon, with the area still restive, with bricks thudding occasionally into streets, with obscenities needling policemen, it became apparent also that most leaders in Harlem were not going to condemn the disorders. Some wanted to use it to make their points. Some were exceedingly angry about police measures the previous night. Some wanted to increase the momentum.

James Farmer, national director of CORE, received a platform on WABC-TV's "Page One" at 2:45 that afternoon, when the topic of an already scheduled appearance

70

was changed to the topical riots. He immediately charged police brutality in repressing the riots.

"I was up there this morning for five hours," he said. "And what I saw was a blood bath. . . . I saw with my own eyes—I saw a woman who walked up to the police and asked for their assistance in getting a taxicab so that she might go home. This woman was shot in the groin and is now in Harlem Hospital. Police dashed into a grocery store and began indiscriminately swinging clubs and beating customers, men, women and children, to the floor."

Under questioning, he admitted he did not see the grocery store episode, but was told about it.

"I saw also police shooting into windows, into tenement houses and into the Theresa Hotel. I myself went into the Theresa Hotel and with the help of the management there entered some of the rooms, saw the bullet holes through the window and the bullet holes in the wall with the bullets still lodged there. If these persons had not been asleep on their bed at the time or had been standing at the window, they might have been other casualties."

Farmer said, quite correctly, that the list of casualties was too low.

". . . Now, I'm not saying that the community, the people in the community of Harlem, were blameless," he continued. "There was bottle-throwing, but when people throw bottles, when they throw bricks, it's the responsibility of the police to arrest, or at least restrain the culprits, the guilty parties, not indiscriminately to shoot into hotel windows and tenement houses. Not to beat people who are merely walking down the street as I saw happen. I saw some young men walking down the street and heard police scream, 'Let's get those niggers,' and then they dashed in. . . . The police were hysterical."

It was on this program that Farmer charged the riot was started by "the inspector at the precinct [who] then screamed, 'I've had enough of this, to hell with those niggers, get them all, arrest them all.'"

He had a kick in passing for Harlem's merchants, also.

"There are economic oppressors in the community which become a target and this is one reason, I'm sure, for the looting, the tension and the resentment that exist there in the community," he said.

One of his interviewers was interested in this. "The looting results from tension, not desire to steal something?" Farmer was asked.

"Well, I think that all things are related," he said. "The desire to steal grows out of tension, grows out of poverty, grows out of a desire to make a killing."

In seeming contradiction, Farmer urged the people of Harlem both to stay off the streets and to attend the Powell funeral that evening.

He also called for the suspension and immediate arrest on suspicion of murder of Lieutenant Gilligan and renewed the standing CORE demand for a civilian review board.

". . . I think if the citizens of Harlem had felt that the incident of the shooting of this youngster Powell would be turned over to a civilian review board whose judgment they could have confidence in, that what happened last night would not have occurred," he said.

He expressed fear about the effect of the riot on the coming Presidential election. "I'm concerned about it because what happened last night will help the cause of Senator Barry Goldwater . . . ," he said at one point.

Asked to tell why the police were "hysterical," as he charged, Farmer said:

". . . Certainly the bottles that are being thrown frighten some of the policemen, and they had a weapon and they used it; some were trigger-happy, and there was also racism, too, because I heard some policemen on corners, seeing two or three Negro youths walking along the streets, say, 'Let's get those niggers.' "

Asked if there was not "inverse racism" in Negro hatred of white policemen, he blamed the feeling on years of brutality shown by police.

One of his questioners said Negroes investigating the Powell shooting shortly after it occurred had yelled, "You God damn' Irish drunken cop." Farmer interrupted him.

"Not a CORE member, I'm sure," he said.

Police were quick to deny most of the charges Farmer had made. But reporters found a woman named Barbara Barksdale, twenty-three, who had been treated at Harlem Hospital for a wound in her left thigh from being hit by a ricocheting bullet as she entered a taxicab. She was treated and released. After the program Farmer admitted that he had not actually seen the shooting, either, but had been told about it.

Both Inspector Pendergast and *Times* reporter Paul Montgomery, witness to the start of the riot, denied that the inspector had used the word "nigger" outside the 28th Precinct stationhouse.

Police Commissioner Murphy hotly denied that police had fired into tenements or the hotel. As for failure to make arrests, he said, each arrest seemed to inflame the crowd and also required that policemen leave the street, where they were needed, to take the prisoners to jail.

But Farmer had had forty-five minutes on television in the afternoon and the rebuttals to his charges didn't get quite the same exposure—at least that day.

73

Those who wanted to increase the momentum appeared in force a little later for a rally called by Jesse Gray, the Harlem rent strike leader, at the Mount Morris Presbyterian Church, southeast of the main part of the previous night's rioting.

There were about five hundred present, half of them black nationalists. Wags like to refer to the Ku Klux Klan as the White Muslims and, in the same spirit, it would be fair to call this a meeting of the Black Citizens Council.

Gray received a standing ovation when he appeared wearing a bandage on his left cheek which he said covered an injury inflicted by a policeman the night before.

"We're about to witness in New York City what we have heard about in Mississippi," he said. "Somebody has said the only thing that will solve the situation in Mississippi is guerrilla warfare. I'm beginning to wonder what will solve the problem here."

A shout came from the audience: "Guerrilla warfare!"

Then came a tirade against police.

"We have one of the most corrupt, rotten police departments in this country," Gray shouted. "Murphy is nothing but a crumb-snatcher and a stoolie. Last night, the police looked better than German Storm Troops."

The crowd understood "better" as irony. "Nazis!" they shouted. "Nazis—that's what they are."

Outside the church, helmeted police stood quietly waiting for the moment when these people would be sent from the church.

Marshall England, head of the New York chapter of CORE, followed Gray to the podium and began an unusually mild speech. He chided the audience for failing to register to vote and was telling them that "Negroes

74

must vote and organize" when he was drowned out by boos and catcalls. England finally retreated from the podium and Gray called on Edward Mills Davis, who was much less temperate.

"You are not going to solve the problem by an emotional outburst or undirected violence," Davis said.

". . . All you young men who know anything about arms and warfare, get ready to make plans to free yourself."

"If we must die, we must die scientifically."

Gray called for "one hundred dedicated men who are ready to die," and volunteers shouted from the audience, "What'll we do? Where'll we go?"

A girl began to pass out blue cards for the volunteers while Gray announced that he would lead a demonstration at the United Nations the next day to ask the UN to intervene in the "police terror" in the United States.

"Let's bomb them," a girl in the audience shouted. "Let's get bombs and destroy them!"

Gray told each of his volunteers, "We're going to make you a platoon captain and you're going to have to get another hundred that are loyal to you. Fifty thousand well-organized Negroes in New York City can determine what happens in New York City."

Herald Tribune reporter Martin G. Berck asked him later why he wanted this large group, and Gray said he was forming a community protection organization.

Isaiah Robinson, head of the Harlem Parents Committee, chided Negro men for "standing by while women and children were beaten last night."

"Before the day is over, we'll separate the boys from the men and the women from the girls," he said. "Stand up like men and die for democracy.

"Some of the press would call this inciting a riot, but when Patrick Henry said, 'Give me liberty or give me death,' nobody called that inciting a riot."

Mention of the press reminded the audience that reporters were present and yells of "Throw them out" started.

James Farmer appeared and was booed until he started speaking of young Powell of "my son and your son and every black man's son" and called for the arrest of Lieutenant Gilligan.

"Let's go," cried the crowd. "What are we waiting for?"

He stopped them by raising his hand. "If you go out of here, one running one way, one running another, throwing bottles, it will be slaughter," he said, and the crowd sat down.

Bayard Rustin, engineer of the March on Washington and of New York's first school boycott, entered with a large crowd of young men and asked for peace, receiving boos. He stared until the crowd became quiet and then said:

"There is nobody in this room who cares more than I do that a young boy was shot down like an animal. . . . There is nobody that has gone to jail more often than I have.

"I am not ready to die. I want no human being to die or be brutalized . . . , but to add to these monstrous deeds is to make an animal of me as the police were animals."

The booing rose to a crescendo and Rustin left the podium. In the rear of the church, part of the crowd started toward him with menacing gestures, but his own followers intervened and he made his way outside. Then he asked for volunteers to help man a command post at 125th Street and Eighth Avenue that night "where we can deploy young men to help disperse teen-agers and give protection to women and children who are on the street."

He obtained about seventy-five volunteers and took them away to make identifying armbands.

It was an ugly crowd that poured out of the church after the rally and, for the next few hours, it would be very dangerous to be an unarmed white man in Harlem. About the only unarmed whites in Harlem were reporters and photographers.

First to feel the wrath of the crowd were Seymour Zee, photographer, and Mike Pearl, reporter, both with the *Journal-American.* Zee stood in the middle of Mount Morris Park West, taking pictures of the crowd as it left the church. Pearl was near him and noticed they were receiving long, hostile looks. But he didn't feel any particular danger until someone shouted, "I don't want you to take my picture."

A young man advanced and the crowd followed. The two white men backed across the street until they were stopped by a parked car. The crowd pressed them against the fender and hood. Zee attempted to placate the hostiles by pointing out that he took pictures of everything he saw, and the two white men began to edge away along the car. This infuriated the mob.

The newspapermen were kicked and kneed. Hands were pressed near their faces in threatening gestures. Pearl felt a hand crack him in the eye. Fingers jabbed into him as men screamed for his attention.

A few feet away, on the other side of the car, stood a double row of policemen unwilling to interfere. Pearl tried not to show fear.

He took notes with trembling hand, attempting to jot down the things being screamed into his face. The notes were jerked from his hand and a voice said, "What are you writing, white boy?"

"Write this," the man commanded. "Write what would

have happened if that police lieutenant was black and that boy white."

The man grabbed Pearl's tie and wrenched his head around. "Look at me, white boy!" he shouted.

Pearl, choking and pressed by the crowd, had decided his time was at hand when he heard a cool voice with an edge of command say, "Give that fellow back his notes." His tie was released. He saw Junius Griffin, a Negro who commands a great deal of personal and professional respect as a reporter for the *New York Times*.

"Why should I?"

"Because they belong to him," said Griffin. The notes were jammed back into Pearl's hand.

Griffin edged up to the two white men and whispered, "Let's get out of this. Follow me. Slow, real slow."

The mob reluctantly gave way before his air of authority.

Pearl's explanation of why police didn't come to his aid was simple. "You get into spots too hot even for the police," he wrote.

The mob in front of the church was not discriminating against reporters solely on the basis of color. A Negro photographer working for a magazine had been told, "You work for the white man, so you're an Uncle Tom." Lester Carson, a Negro who is a reporter for the *World-Telegram and Sun*, was standing nearby and quietly removed his press badge. After that, Negro reporters working for general circulation dailies did not wear the badges. Eddie Cumberbatch, of the *Post*, showed his as furtively as an FBI agent flashing his credentials. Carson said he showed his badge only when police charged a crowd of which he was a member. "Then I held it in my teeth," he said.

But, as a Negro, Carson had some advantages now. He was able to follow the crowd as it drifted up to the Levy and Delany Funeral Home, where services for young Powell were to begin at 8 P.M. A member of the crowd threw a bottle at police stationed in the area, a policeman threw it back, and Carson decided it was time to get out his credentials. As soon as his press card came out, a rioter grabbed it and ran.

Carson started after him. A voice yelled, "Hold it right there, buddy," It was a policeman, his hand on his revolver, his eyes fixed on the reporter. Carson froze, then got police help in retrieving his credentials.

The funeral home became the center of action. Police had massed behind barricades at the intersection. About a thousand Negroes gathered, looking for trouble. Shortly before the services started, bottles were heaved into police ranks, the crowd began to pour around the barricades, and the battle was on.

Police charged the crowd and three buses pulled up to disgorge TPF riot-breakers. Bottles and bricks rained from rooftops, windows, and the crowd. Every bar on Seventh Avenue closed automatically. Carson, racing for shelter, found a door closed and locked and the manager shouting, "Hide someplace else. I wouldn't open this door for Jesus."

It was a tough place to be a reporter or a photographer. John Orris, a photographer for the *New York Times*, was felled by a blow to his eye and suffered serious facial injuries. Robert Daley, a camerman for Columbia Broadcasting System, was charged by a mob of young men. His crew scattered to safety, but Daley was knocked down and beaten with fists and clubs; his arm was broken. Tuck Stadler, a reporter for Radio Station WINS, had a lighted cigarette ground into the back of his neck. The unarmed press corps was suffering a higher ratio of injuries than the Police Department. Its members, heretofore reluctant to identify themselves with the police, began to mooch helmets, sacrificing their appearance of neutrality for head protection.

The press corps, ever favorable to the underdog, also was beginning to find its sympathies with the cops. Farmer's comment that the people of Harlem were not blameless for the bloodshed seemed the understatement of the year, even to very liberal reporters. The Negroes had gone too far.

The battle raged along the avenue even during the funeral.

The Bronx boy's funeral was being held in Harlem because he had attended St. Augustine's Baptist Church there.

Inside the funeral home, about one hundred mourners listened as Jimmy Powell's minister, the Reverend Theodore Kerrison, delivered a eulogy. As he began the twenty-third Psalm, the crash of breaking bottles and a volley of shots could be heard from outside.

Mrs. Annie Powell, mother of the dead boy, was helped from the funeral home near collapse. A sound truck drew up and Bayard Rustin climbed aboard.

"I urge you to go home," he said. "We know there has been an injustice done. The thing we need to do most is respect this woman whose son was shot."

"Uncle Tom!" the crowd shouted. "Tom! Uncle Tom!"

Rustin was unmoved. "I'm prepared to be a Tom if it's the only way I can save women and children from being shot down in the street, and if you're not willing to do the same, you're fools!" He was roundly booed.

Other speakers followed him on the sound truck, with no more success. They continued to tour the area, however, pleading with the mob to disperse.

Bricks and bottles were coming down 130th Street and police began to herd the mob away, firing in the air. A Molotov cocktail came out of the crowd and fell into the street, its flames leaping up. At least some of the police then lowered their guns to shoot to kill, and two young men fell wounded as the police charged. Gunsmoke began to hang heavy over the avenue as police tried to break up the crowds and to drive the brick-throwers back from the roofs. The TPF finally cleared the roofs, and the crowd was herded away in segments, still hurling its missiles and defiance, spreading the disorder.

Police had blocked traffic from much of the area and the small battles raged through playgrounds, housing projects, over to Eighth Avenue and to Lenox and down south of 125th Street. Store windows crashed again and the sound of burglar alarms became familiar, but not as familiar as on Saturday night.

By midnight, the violence was sporadic; but a new disturbance flared as police guided a fire engine along 124th Street. Bricks and bottles began to come from rooftops. The fighting started again and two men were wounded by bullets. A detective collapsed with a heart attack.

A couple of hours later, in the same block, Molotov cocktails were being thrown and one went into a second floor apartment, where it set fire to a woman's dress. Firemen got to the fire quickly and the woman was sent to Harlem Hospital for treatment of burns.

But, by 1:30 A.M., the Police Department had declared the situation under control.

Detective Inspector Thomas Renaghan, deploying his forces from the men's wash room of a shelter in Mount Morris Park, had one large doubt about that, though, when he heard a noise behind him. He swung from his make-shift desk and found a Negro using the urinal. "What are you doing here?" he roared. "What does it look like I'm doing?" asked the visitor. "Get out! Get out of my office!" said the inspector with as much force as he could muster while suppressing laughter.

Summing up the day, reporters liked to remember the sight of policemen playing with small Negro children or chatting in friendly fashion with Negro waitresses in the few restaurants which dared to remain open. It seemed indisputable that most of the residents of Harlem were not particularly mad at anybody, except the rioters who were making all that fuss and causing all that trouble. Yet, they did condemn the shooting of young Powell, and their argument generally was that a grown policeman should have been able to disarm a fifteen-year-old without killing him.

It was only a few hours before some of the force was taken out of that argument. At 5:15 A.M. Monday, Patrolman James Lanzano, twenty-nine, off-duty and in civilian clothes, saw a man threatening another man with a knife near Times Square. He and another off-duty patrolman, Edward Wrage, chased the man and cornered him. Both drew their guns. Lanzano moved in to disarm the man and the knife flashed into his throat. Wrage managed to staunch the bleeding and the patrolman's life was saved at a hospital, but the point was not lost on his family.

"I guess Jim just thought twice before he decided not to shoot," said his brother, Thomas. "I don't know why he didn't use his gun. I believe policemen today are almost afraid to use their guns . . . look what happened to Lieutenant Gilligan."

Farmer, still calling for peace, also was appealing for

82

Governor Nelson A. Rockefeller to send the National Guard to "protect the citizens of Harlem."

The official toll now was 27 policemen and 93 civilians injured (hospitals reported treating more than 200), 108 arrested, and 45 stores damaged or looted.

5

Monday, July 20

Peter Kane, manager of the A & P Supermarket on Eighth Avenue at 131st Street, spent Monday morning surveying the damage from Sunday night's riot. A seventy-five-foot pane of glass, costing $1,500, had been shattered, $500 worth of merchandise had been stolen. He pointed to a scorched place on the floor. "Molotov cocktail," he said. "We wouldn't have a store here today if police hadn't put out the fire with grapefruit juice. It's the best use I've ever found for grapefruit juice."

He should have boarded up that window, but he couldn't know that.

At 130th Street and Lenox, a young man watched repairmen working on the windows of a looted bar and a cleaning shop.

"They shouldn't have broken into the cleaners and took those clothes," he said. "They were just harming the people who live in this neighborhood. I don't care about the bar. It's owned by a whitey, anyway."

At 9 A.M., about one hundred policemen were on duty

in front of the Levy and Delany Funeral Home, and a comparatively small, very quiet crowd was gathered. A long, black limousine drew up and the Powell family got out of it. Police helped the undertaker clear a path for the family, then moved away. A police helicopter hovered over the scene. The family came back out of the funeral home following the coffin, and a thin Negro woman in the crowd lost her self-control. She lunged at a white policeman, shouting, "Oh, why did they have to shoot the boy?" A Negro man pulled her back, saying, "There's nothing you can do."

Mrs. Powell, her head thrown back, cried, "Oh, my baby, my baby," and was helped back into the limousine. A six-vehicle procession started the trip to Hartsdale, N.Y., where the boy was buried next to his father, Harold, who had died a few years before.

The Reverend Theodore Kerrison read a graveside service, interrupted once by the mother, who cried, "Oh, Harold, Harold, look how they've sent you my baby!"

Harlem was peaceful. Most of the action was vocal and taking place elsewhere.

Acting Mayor Screvane and Commissioner Murphy had met early with two separate civil rights groups; neither group received more than a sympathetic hearing of its requests, which included assignment of Negro policemen to Harlem. Police considered this an interesting reversal. Civil rights groups had once protested "segregation" of Negro police to Harlem on the grounds that Negro officers were good enough to work anywhere.

Showing up as the principal demand, however, was that for the civilian review board, for which civil rights groups had long been asking. Voices were joining them now, subscribing to the theory that existence of such a board might have prevented the riots.

In Washington, both Senator Jacob E. Javits, New York Republican, and Representative William Fitts Ryan, Manhattan Democrat, called for establishment of a civilian review board. The executive committee of the New York County (Manhattan) Democratic organization voted unanimously to ask Mayor Wagner to establish the board by executive order.

The Police Community Relations Board of East Harlem called for a special Council meeting to enact the bill. The Social Action Committee of Grace Congregational Church made a similar appeal. The Workers Defense League expressed its support of the Weiss Bill. So did the Uptown Tenants Council. The seventy-five Negro minister members of the Interdenominational Ministers Alliance of Brooklyn and Long Island proposed appointment of a minister in each block of Central Harlem to act as liaison between residents and police.

Commissioner Murphy had fought the proposal for such a board on the grounds that the effect would be to "create situations where policemen would hesitate to act, fearful of the second-guessers, and the Monday-morning quarterbacks." Now, the pressure was on.

"The Negro in this city needs to be protected from the police," said the Reverend Joseph H. May, pastor of Mount Carmel Baptist Church, Rockaway Beach. "Where the Negro has asked for the bread of justice, he had been given a stone. The stationing of so many policemen in Harlem inflames the people. This is not Commissioner Murphy's fortress."

The Reverend Dr. Dan M. Potter, executive director of the Protestant Council of New York, asked that public meetings be kept at a minimum in Harlem to avoid further heightening of tension.

"Mob rule must not be permitted to replace the courts in the solution of complicated community problems," he said.

A. Philip Randolph, president of the Negro-American Labor Council and a fifty-year resident of Harlem, appealed for peace.

"Violence and bloodshed is not the remedy," he said. "It will destroy our community and hurt and set back the Negro cause. It only plays into the hands of our enemies. It could elect Senator Goldwater, who voted against civil rights legislation, President, which would be the greatest disaster to befall Negroes since slavery. Since there is now a Federal civil rights law, let us declare a moratorium on demonstrations and peacefully test it and work for its enforcement."

Many other stable citizens of Harlem shared the venerable labor leader's attitude, but there were those who felt otherwise.

Their public announcement appeared on the streets of Harlem on Monday in the form of a blue leaflet signed by the Harlem Defense Council and Jesse Gray's Community Council on Housing.

The leaflets called for support of Gray's demonstration at 6 P.M. outside the United Nations to protest "terrorism and genocide committed against Black Americans."

They also urged residents to organize for the purpose "of defending each and every block" in Harlem from the cops.

"The events of the last two days have shown that if we are not organized, we are just a mob and are not in a position to deal with the enemy," the leaflets said.

Then they urged Harlemites to support a mass rally on the next Saturday in front of the 32nd Precinct, on

West 135th Street. This was unpleasantly reminiscent of the beginning of the riots on the previous Saturday at the 28th Precinct.

The Harlem Defense Council was a new organization, but it didn't take long to determine it was sharing offices with the Progressive Labor Party, headed by William Epton, who described himself as a follower of the Chinese Communists.

By evening, concessions were being made by the city. Screvane announced that a New York County grand jury would begin its investigation of the Powell killing the next day and that Mayor Wagner had canceled the rest of his European tour and was flying back to New York. The grand jury would have investigated the shooting anyway, policemen said. But this investigation was believed opening earlier than usual; in fact, authorities still had not rounded up all the witnesses.

Screvane, who had spent the entire day in consultations, said everyone he talked to regretted the bloodshed "in an outbreak which is projected to the world as reflecting shame and discredit on New York City and the United States.

"Racists and demagogues in our city and elsewhere in the United States benefit by such an outbreak and such a display," he said. "All other citizens are the losers. Peace, order and constructive action must be the order of the day."

Then he announced the following new programs:

▶ Deputy Mayor Edward F. Cavanagh would review procedures of the Police Department's civilian complaint review board.

▶ Commissioner Murphy would assign additional Negro officers and patrolmen to Harlem.

▶ A new Community Affairs Committee of top police officials, including Murphy, would meet regularly with community leaders.

▶ An intensive program of recruiting and "pre-training" members of minority groups for the police force would begin.

▶ Channels of communication between minority communities and City Hall would be expanded through city offices already located in the neighborhoods.

In spite of the inflammatory leaflets, Harlem had remained quiet through the afternoon, with most residents going about their normal business. The trouble waited until after the UN demonstration.

About two hundred white and Negro pickets marched in that demonstration and they displayed posters similar to police "wanted" flyers, featuring a picture of Lieutenant Gilligan, topped by "WANTED FOR MURDER" and, below, "GILLIGAN, THE COP. Lieutenant Thomas Gilligan of the 14th Division." The posters were signed "Harlem Defense Council, 336 Lenox Ave., N.Y.C., FI 8-2254." The posters appeared in Harlem shortly after the rally. Youngsters began to parade them along 125th Street, and they were seen on the sides of automobiles until traffic was finally stopped later in the evening.

Shortly before sunset, the third night of rioting began. Negroes ambling up and down Seventh Avenue near 125th Street threw bottles at policemen. They were dispersed with nightsticks, not gunfire. Small fires were set in trash cans and buildings, and firemen began an endless night of running through the streets of Harlem. A drugstore window was broken at Seventh Avenue and 125th Street.

By 9 P.M., it was obvious that the rioting in Harlem had not screeched to a halt, as it had in 1943. Tension was still heavy in the air, but policemen were thick along the streets. It seemed very doubtful that a full-scale riot could develop, much as many people might have wanted it to. An eerie silence prevailed at 125th Street and Lenox Avenue, where crowds were thick, but civilian traffic was absent. The usual roar of Manhattan had dwindled. A dog could be heard barking in the distance, just as he could have been heard in a small town.

The crowds moving along the sidewalks were not riotous-looking types. A high percentage of the people were well dressed and many towed neatly dressed children behind them, apparently bringing them to 125th Street to see the excitement. There was excitement, too. The silence suddenly was shattered by the passage of a couple of dozen police cars, which whizzed north on Lenox, stopped briefly, then returned, their sirens silent. As they neared 125th, shots were fired around the corner and a crowd of young teen-agers raced around and ducked down into the IRT subway entrance, to be shooed back out by Transit Authority police who were holding the station.

Along 125th Street, where helmeted policemen were stationed only a few feet apart, there was constant provocation and continuous restraint. The pet Negro obscenity, an accusation of incest which turns middle-class stomachs, was being thrown into the faces of both Negro and white policemen, quietly and casually, by nearly every Negro who passed. Police were past hearing.

Further east, at Second Avenue, police were shooting into the air to break up a mob of about a thousand people. Chanting crowds marched and countermarched along the streets and, by 10 P.M., the center of interest had shifted to the block of 125th Street between Eighth Avenue and St. Nicholas Avenue, which contains New York

CORE headquarters, several African Nationalist offices, the Harlem Labor Center, and assorted bars, restaurants, and hot dog stands. The hot dog stands were still in business, but the bars had locked their doors, and the help sneered when customers applied for admission. Fire apparatus was being used to block 125th Street between Amsterdam Avenue and Fifth Avenue and also Lenox and Seventh Avenues between 116th and 135th Streets, so, except for police cars which whizzed by occasionally on the way to assist officers in trouble, the street was free to pedestrian traffic.

Hundreds of Negroes were gathered on the corners of Eighth Avenue, and hundreds more stood on the sidewalks on both sides of the street in front of CORE headquarters. Police moved the crowds on the west end of the block, and a young well-dressed Negro women shouted through a megaphone, "You don't have to run; you live here." The crowds kept moving and police kept following them. A young man wearing a black armband spotted the press badge on a reporter—Sullivan—and lectured him on who was not involved in the rioting. "The Muslims aren't doing this," he said. "The Muslims are a nonviolent organization." Ben Holman, CBS-TV reporter who was beaten a year before while covering a Muslim meeting in Harlem, two men beaten at a Muslim rally before the eyes of policemen a few weeks before, and the followers of the dissident Malcolm X would have contradicted him on this. Policemen agreed that the crowd on the block was undoubtedly hostile, but they said it did not appear to be as dangerous as the one at the funeral home the night before.

Teen-agers caught the eye. They stood in obscenity-shouting crowds near a policeman, finally threw bottles, then stampeded with shrieks of glee when the police charged. This was bull-running—fun of the kind seen in Pamplona, Spain, where daring youngsters and adults run through the streets before the fighting bulls. It added immensely to the Hallowe'en air of the block and brought a curse from a Negro police sergeant. "Where the hell are those kids' parents?" he asked. "They must have some kind of parents. Don't they care what they do?"

The reporter made his way to a telephone booth on the northeast corner and, as he edged through the crowd, heard a voice at his shoulder say, "You'll get it, too, white man." Wheeling, he saw a well-dressed Negro walking ahead, his face impassive, giving no sign of the threat just uttered.

In the middle of the block, ranking police officers gathered across from CORE headquarters and well-dressed men popped out of the crowd to shout excitedly at them that the presence of the police was raising the people's emotions. "Get all those police out of here and they'll settle down," was the impassioned message frequently delivered. Photographer Nat Fein, of the *Herald Tribune*, stood on the south side of the street and complained with some bitterness that a man had thrown a bottle at him. A moment later, another bottle came out of the crowd and landed near a cop. The cops charged, the mob stampeded with shrieks and a man stumbled. Stumbling when fleeing the police that night meant a couple of whacks on the head from a nightstick. A policeman administered them and walked back to his post, and the man sat up on the sidewalk.

Across 125th Street from CORE headquarters raced a Negro youth in an Army helmet liner crudely lettered with the words "First Aid." He knelt beside the injured man and tenderly examined his knee, although that was not where he had been hit. The aidman did something and went back across the street. The wounded man rose to his feet and walked away, scowling. He easily could have been an innocent who was trying to get through the crowd when it stampeded.

It was about that time that Ted Jones of the *Times,* who is a Negro, witnessed the beating of two innocents near the Theresa Hotel. The TPF stampeded a crowd of teen-agers and two Negro men were caught, bewildered, in the rush. The TPF was on them, flailing vigorously with clubs, and Jones, a native of Harlem, decided this was too much. His indignant yells to stop beating those men caused a diminutive policeman to turn on him, but his press badge saved him from any more than being pushed to the pavement and receiving an order to leave the area. Jones, furious, came back with reinforcements from the press corps and ostentatiously took the policeman's badge number. He never registered a formal complaint, but he was pleased "to worry that little so-and-so." He was very interested to learn later that the two innocent men he had seen beaten were police plainclothesmen.

Things were still lively back at Eighth Avenue.

A Negro youth with an armband lettered "CORE" walked through the crowd, shouting into a walkie-talkie of the type sold in department stores. He said he was working in crowd control for CORE, but he had no time to explain this. A crowd came marching west on 125th Street from Seventh Avenue, waving the Gilligan posters and chanting, "Killer cops must go!" Police turned them back and they marched away. Now, Nat Fein and a couple of policemen were struck by BB's. They believed they had been fired from the upper windows of a building next to

CORE. They cautioned their friends not to look at the window if they valued their eyesight.

Through the crowd came the large figure of Bayard Rustin, announcing that he had to get to the precinct. Deputy Chief Inspector Pierce Glynn offered to take him and asked what the trouble was. "There's a group leaving Times Square that must be stopped," Rustin said. "You must stop them." He conferred with the police official, who then moved over to a radio car and gave some instructions. The reporter buttonholed Rustin and asked him what the crowd was. "I just know it has to be stopped," Rustin said and moved away.

A bottle sailed out of the crowd at CORE, and four patrolmen yanked a man out of the group, rushed him across the street, and threw him into a squad car, banging his head on the top of the car in the process. Well-dressed men immediately rushed up to police officials and entered vehement protests. "We were just talking him into going home," one of them shouted. Police finally released him and he was led away, looking dazed. A boy with a walkie-talkie jogged across 125th Street, heading south on Eighth Avenue. Trotting beside him, her hand hooked to his arm and her face shining up at his was a small teen-age girl. It began to occur to some people that a great many of the people of Harlem were enjoying this situation; it was much better drama than any of the television reruns, and there was much opportunity for audience participation.

A drunken Negro reeled about in the center of the street and eyed a police car making a U-turn. "You want war?" he shouted. "We'll give you war. Wait'll the Puerto Ricans come over to help us. They'll be over tonight." Everyone ignored him.

Into this bedlam drove a police sound truck. The policeman inside began to recite over and over: "Attention, Mr. Overton requests your presence in 312." About three hundred men filed up into the Harlem Labor Center at 312 West 125th Street and heard Joseph Overton urge that they end the riots and take their grievances to City Hall. "All you're doing here is tearing up your own stores, your own property," he said. At the end of the short speech, they filed back down to the street and across to CORE headquarters, where Farmer stood and harangued them, urging them to go home.

From the fringe of this crowd came occasional shouts of "Freedom!"

But Farmer, Rustin, and Overton moved away from CORE, and the crowd, several hundred strong, followed them. In the center of the street, Captain Lloyd Sealy, a Negro who later was to receive command of the 28th Precinct, told a superior officer, "Farmer's going to move them away from here. We'd better let them go."

The crowd moved west to St. Nicholas Avenue, marched around the intersection once, and then turned north, chanting, "We want justice." The marchers were followed by wary policemen. Sullivan descended into the IND subway station, found a telephone, and was filling in his rewriteman when he heard shots. He ran from the station just as a little boy tumbled down the steps and huddled at the bottom, saying, wide-eyed, "They're shootin' people."

Near 128th Street, policemen were firing into the air. "They started throwing bottles," one of them explained. A bottle crashed into the police lines and the shooting started again. Sullivan ducked behind a car and a dark figure in a white helmet liner dived to join him, shouting, "First aid, first aid." It was the teen-ager aidman and he meant "Non-combatant, non-combatant." The crowd was driven off by the gunshots, and Sullivan found that his press badge had attracted about ten Negroes, who said they were newspapermen. They explained that Farmer had been trying to lead the crowd away "and the cops spoiled it with all that shooting." Farmer was marching back toward 125th Street, looking very indignant.

Few newspapermen had cared to approach the crowd in front of CORE and those who had were quickly discouraged by venomous looks and words. Gay Talese, of the *New York Times*, had actually walked through the crowd and into CORE's upstairs headquarters at about 10 P.M. He found that CORE had locked three white members, two women and Henry Schwarzschild, in a back room to protect them from the Negro mob. Schwarzschild, a veteran civil rights worker who had been jailed with Negroes after demonstrations in Jackson, Mississippi, in 1961 and at the New York World's Fair in 1964, found this more than a little ironic, but took a philosophical attitude. Talese was locked in with them, warned that "the situation is mad down there," and not released until 11 P.M., when he and the others were escorted to a waiting taxi.

His story of his imprisonment for his own protection surprised several reporters and photographers who had been standing in the street during that period, suffering no more than an occasional badly aimed bottle and bursts of vilification. Nick Thimmesch, a correspondent for *Time* magazine, had even needled the other reporters about the police helmets which most of them were wearing. His own blond head looked very bare as it towered above most of the crowd, but not a hair of it was hurt. Ironically, Wally Terry, a Negro correspondent for *Time,* was felled by a brick.

A half block east on 125th Street, a waitress in a restaurant discussed the situation with a Negro customer.

"Jesse Gray says all of us should go on strike and stay away from work," she said. Her customer grunted in disgust.

"If Jesse Gray wants to pay my bills, I'll stay away from work," he said.

By 11 P.M., the sound of sirens was almost continuous as streams of squad cars raced from one reported incident to another, most of them false reports, and hollow-eyed, scowling firemen who should have been in their beds raced from one fire alarm to another, most of them also false. About midnight, a Molotov cocktail crashed through the window of a pharmacy, touching off a fire. Police grabbed a twenty-seven-year-old who had arrived in New York from South Carolina two weeks before and charged him with arson. A joyful crowd gathered at the corner, cheering the fire and booing the firemen, who fingered their axes.

Sullivan was telephoning from a booth across the street in a gas-station drive when a squad of policemen marched past the scene of the fire on the way to relieve the day shift. The crowd began to jeer them by counting cadence. The police ignored them until a bottle crashed into the street; then they gripped their clubs and turned to glare, but kept marching. A few minutes later, the men they had relieved came marching down Eighth Avenue. Another bottle was thrown, and the men staged one last charge, firing into the air and swinging their clubs. The reporter's telephone booth had been safe because two policemen were standing nearby, but they joined the charge. Immediately, several Negroes crowded in front of the door and began to interview the reporter, who was, because of the nature of telephone booths, their prisoner.

Good humor seemed called for and he joked with them, discussing how lousy cops are, until he could edge his hypocritical way through them to a point within reach of one of those lousy, lovely, armed cops. Then he gabbed with the Negroes for a while and discovered that at least two of them were Brooklynites, in Harlem "for the foon [fun]."

At Eighth Avenue and 123rd Street, a bar looked safe, and Sullivan entered it. A woman stood inside, gazing out the window and wishing vocally that she had the nerve to go home. The bartender told her to walk fast to 125th Street, catch the crosstown bus and hope for the best. The reporter suspected there were thousands of people in Harlem business places who were afraid to go home that night.

The 28th Precinct was a hive of activity as men from other precincts and boroughs reported in, received their assignments and marched out. When Sullivan walked back to Eighth Avenue, he found the safe-looking bar closed. He learned later that its owner had seen police charge into a bar across the street, and had watched that bar wrecked in the ensuing fight. Polite questioning revealed that the raided bar's patrons had been running out, heaving bottles at police, then running back in locking the door. Police had tired of this sport.

At 126th Street, a brick went through a jewelry store window and the man who tossed it was grabbed by police while he was still reaching in for the loot. They threw him in a car and had started to make a U-turn when he leaned out the window to shout, "Help me, brothers." The crowd closed in and freed him. Police hadn't even obtained his name.

At 125th Street and Lenox Avenue, eight Negro youths extended the action to the IRT subway. They boarded a southbound train and began shoving and punching passengers. Transit Authority policemen were waiting for them at the 96th Street station and hauled them back to Harlem, for booking.

By 1 A.M., the crowds had thinned perceptibly, the sirens were no longer continuous, and the gunfire had died down. Then shots sounded up Eighth Avenue and squad cars roared from every direction, their dome lights flashing and sirens screaming. The scene became eerie. Nearly forty rotating red lights lined up neatly north of 126th Street. Gunfire broke loose, heavy as an infantry attack, although all the weapons were pistols—or nearly all of them. Two World War II veterans racing up the avenue saw what could only be tracer bullets floating up from the street. No one has been able to explain this, except to say that someone in that swarm of policemen may have had a carbine.

The center of this activity was a place called Sam's West Side Bar, across from the St. Nicholas Houses project and just below the A & P which had been broken into the night before. Sullivan and a newsreel photographer from United Press International panted up to the bar as a swarm of policemen gathered in front.

Glass shattered and they disappeared inside. Thuds, bangs, and yells came from within; the front window crumbled into the street, and a man shot through the door and landed in a heap on the sidewalk. It was a scene from a Grade B movie. The police came out and assembled in the street.

A Negro walked out of the bar into the center of the street, marched down toward 130th, made it to the corner, and fell backward into the street, where he lay motionless.

Television cameras were very much in evidence now

and floodlights were turned on him. The group of Negroes who had said they were newspapermen buttonholed reporters and screamed "Look! Look! Look what those cops did! Look at this police brutality!"

Another man walked from the bar down the sidewalk and crumpled up in a doorway, bleeding from the head. Suddenly, into the glare of the floodlight in the street strode a very short, very muscular Negro wearing a pork-pie hat. From under the hat streams of blood trickled down the front, back, and both sides of his head. Television cameras swung his way.

"I just got off work," he raged. "I just had one drink and I was sitting there and I got this!"

"Animals!" screamed the chorus. "That's what they are! Animals!"

A huge Negro in an apron, Sam's bartender, was now being treated by CORE's first-aid kid. The boy wound a turban around his split head as the bartender denounced the police. "People were throwing bricks off the roof and we locked the door so we wouldn't get involved, but they broke through the door and came in hitting and shooting and wrecking the place."

A brick from the roof landed in the street with a sickening thud. The fusillade began again. When it died, Sullivan found the A & P just north of the bar. Behind the huge, jagged remnants of that $1,500 store front were two helmeted patrolmen, who pointed to a rubbish can on the floor. "They threw that through the window," one said. "We were in here guarding the place and they were threatening to come in after us. A squad car was standing by and called for help and they ran into the bar."

"Watch it," said the other patrolman. "They're throwing bricks."

Almost as if he had given a signal, bricks began to hit the pavement with a force that broke them into flying fragments, a little like artillery shells. Gunfire started again. Sullivan crouched by the store front, feeling relatively safe until he remembered the menacing pieces of plate glass above him. He scuttled in a soldier's crouch to a doorway. The door was closed, but he bumped it and it moved slightly. From inside, a tremulous voice said, "Ain't nobody in here but women." "Nobody out here but a reporter," he said, and pushed the door open. A middle-aged woman and a young woman were huddled inside. "We were just going by on our way home when they threw some bricks, and the police went in and wrecked that bar," said one of the women. "Do you suppose it's safe to go now?" It looked safe and they scurried across the street and down Eighth Avenue.

A police sergeant explained: "The gang that had been threatening the two men in the A & P ran into the bar when we got here. Then the bricks came off the roof and we had to clear it. When the men went to the bar, the door was locked and someone threw a bottle through it at them, so they went in."

The CORE kid said three of the four injured men were shot. An ambulance had come up and was taking the injured away. "I saw one's brains hanging out," the kid said —an erroneous report. None of the men was seriously injured.

The bartender, colorful in his turban, was displaying a broken nightstick through the smashed window for the benefit of television cameras. "Get the number off it," someone yelled. "You can find out who it belonged to."

Sullivan walked inside to find the bar looking like debris from a tornado. The air was heavy with the smell of liquor sloshing amid broken glass and a tangle of stools behind the bar.

"Who threw the stools back there?" the bartender was asked.

"Those ——— cops!" was the answer. "They came in hittin' and throwin' things. They're animals!"

There was a perfectly good telephone in a perfectly friendly barbecue restaurant a block down Eighth Avenue, but now Sullivan saw two telephones in the back of the barroom. They tempted him and he succumbed. He was telling a rewriteman the facts when bricks hit the pavement again and shooting started outside. It threw the twenty Negroes in the bar into a rage. The reporter slid by reflex down to the floor of the telephone booth and heard a voice shout, "We gotta kill all those ——— whiteys!" There was no doubt that he was a whitey and the only one in the bar.

He rose, leaving the telephone dangling. The patrons had massed at the door and window. No back door could be seen, although there was a back room occupied by a very frightened Negro. The reporter went forward, reached the crowd and gently pushed his way through. "Excuse me, gents. Pardon me, buddy. Can I get through, fellas." He made the sidewalk undamaged. But the sidewalk was not safety. He glimpsed two teen-agers kneeling behind a truck. One of them guiltily dropped a bottle at the sight of the white helmet, but the other, kneeling next to the truck's gas tank, stared insolently and went right on stuffing a rag into the neck of a fluid-filled bottle.

As the nearest target, Sullivan felt it would be foolhardy to warn the cops on the other side of the truck. He walked in businesslike fashion to the crowd of Negroes who had gathered at 130th Street, expecting at every step to be doused with flaming gasoline. He was safe in the crowd when the firebomb arched over the truck and narrowly missed the UPI Newsfilm man, the father of six and unemployed since his job folded at Cape Kennedy. He was getting his first night's work in several months.

Police began to clear out the crowd. In the barbecue restaurant, customers looked out the door and shook their heads, then went back to their stools and resumed eating, returning the greetings of the whiteys who wandered through to the telephone.

The TPF was on hand now. Slowly it herded the crowds north and south on Eighth Avenue, east through the housing project and west down 130th Street. Mostly, it was deliberate, menacing movement toward the crowds; occasionally there were a charge and a couple of shots. Finally the area cleared except for little boys and drunks who somehow kept penetrating the police lines and were yelled at for their pains. The TPF lined up along Eighth Avenue, took over the roofs, and ordered people to pull their heads back into the tenements.

Peace was returning when a sergeant in a radio car looked up worriedly and said, "They've got a 10-41 in Brooklyn."

A 10-41 is a call for reinforcements.

What part of Brooklyn?

"Bedford-Stuyvesant," he said.

6

Bedford-Stuyvesant

Bedford-Stuyvesant, the *New York Times* said in a head-line, is an "area defined by race."

If that is true, then this ghetto in North Central Brook-lyn is even larger than the population of "nearly 400,000" ascribed to the area by the *Times* in the story. The prob-lem in defining Bedford-Stuyvesant is the same problem as defining Harlem. Your definition depends on where you live, and nobody wants to live in what has become Bed-ford-Stuyvesant. Daniel Diggs, who represents the area in City Council, refuses even to use the name. He wants to go back to calling it Stuyvesant Heights which is what the eastern segment of the area was called before the great Negro migration swept into Bedford-Stuyvesant be-tween the world wars. That migration, greatly reinforced in the past ten years, has been driving out the white com-munity before it as it spreads north in Williamsburg, north-east to Bushwick, southeast to annex Brownsville, south to swallow up nearly half the area once considered fash-ionable Crown Heights, and west to link up with Clinton

Hill and Fort Greene. Assemblyman Thomas R. Jones, who represents one of the two Bedford-Stuyvesant districts in the Assembly, compared the growth of the neighborhood to "those things you see in a microscope when two bodies merge into one big blob." He isn't far wrong.

Estimates of the size of the population of what is now considered Bedford-Stuyvesant range anywhere from the 248,765 reported by the 1960 census-takers—restricted by their refusal to recognize absorption of many of the bordering communities—up to Mr. Jones's: "I've been telling people for years there were half a million Negroes, and the flight of the white people is making things worse, more desperate."

If you take the area now generally considered Bedford-Stuyvesant by nearly all Brooklynites, bounded on the north by Flushing Avenue, the south by Eastern Parkway, the east by Broadway (and a depressing elevated) and the west by Washington Avenue, the population is probably just over 400,000. This geographical definition has its own quirks, too. It includes, for instance, famous old Pratt Institute, up in the northwest corner, and a well-kept middle-class housing development called Willoughby Walk, both of which are generally considered out of Bedford-Stuyvesant; and yet the same boundaries exclude the Fort Greene Houses, probably the borough's most crime-troubled development. Most Brooklynites will swear that Fort Greene is "in" Bedford-Stuyvesant.

New York City police officials do not like to give out crime figures for neighborhoods or precincts, yet reporters like the *Herald Tribune*'s Sam Rubenstein, who has been covering Brooklyn since 1917, says Bedford-Stuyvesant is now the leader in New York City crime. "Now we get murders down there, we cover 'em by phone, we hardly

BEDFORD-STUYVESANT

ever go down there any more. The papers aren't interested in Negro murders."

Inspector Walter Clerke, deputy commander of Brooklyn's Patrol Borough North, simplifies Bedford-Stuyvesant even further as everything in the borough north of Eastern Parkway and east of Flatbush Avenue, which gives it about one quarter of the area of Brooklyn and about one third of the borough's more than 2.6 million residents. It also makes it, just about by common consent, the largest Negro ghetto in the Northern United States, and until Tuesday, July 21, the most unknown.

Then editors all over the world who had been featuring Harlem riot stories for three days and were primed for more, found themselves confronted with a new place name (one much harder to fit into headlies) in Bedford-Stuyvesant. It was small wonder there was some confusion, especially among Americans and Europeans who correlated the name Harlem with the word *ghetto* and the New York City residence of Negroes. As the rioting progressed onto even a larger scale than Harlem, the question arose as to where Bedford-Stuyvesant had been all these years while newspapers were playing stories of racial conflict and crime in Harlem.

The answer, of course, is that it had been right there, growing, from Colonial days. In 1660, one "Francisco the Negro" was listed as a patentee of Bostwyck, which later evolved into Bushwick across Broadway on the northeastern border of Bedford-Stuyvesant. Slavery did not last long in New York State—it finally ended in 1827—but before that, Ralph Foster Weld reports in his *Brooklyn Is America* "more than a thousand Negro men and boys were among the 'patriotic diggers' who constructed entrenchments . . . during the War of 1812." In the Revolutionary War, incidentally, much of the fighting in the Battle of Long Island was conducted along what is now considered Bedford.

The Bedford area itself had come into being in 1663 when fifteen residents asked permission "to form a hamlet there among ourselves to protect the property." Soon, dwellers on farms in what is now northwestern Queens began detouring through Bedford as the logical way of avoiding the creeks and swamps of Wallabout while traveling to the New York ferry.

The first Negro settlers did not start heading that way, however, until the first part of the nineteenth century, when they spread into what was then an undeveloped area east on Fulton Street. It was in 1819 that Brooklyn Negroes held their first demonstration as Negroes when they marched in a group from the Sands Street Methodist Church where a pro-slavery pastor held forth, and formed their own branch of the African Methodist Episcopal Church. There was another demonstration, and a parade, in 1827, when the last vestiges of slavery were finally snuffed out by law.

Significantly, although Negroes in Brooklyn had publicly and eloquently drafted a proclamation decrying several "Return to Africa" movements prevalent at the time, Brooklyn Negroes in the late 1820's also took their children out of the white school to form their own segregated school.

Still, the area which is now Bedford-Stuyvesant was rural, and completely white. What is now Fulton Street was not laid out until 1848. More streets began appearing in the vicinity thereafter, but even by 1880, a painting of the landscape at Bedford Corners displayed at the Brooklyn Library shows a completely rural crossroads.

Because of the social advantages and beauty of the area, however, it soon began attracting real-estate interest. "In the latter part of the century," Brooklyn historian Nicholas Marlow says, "row after row of splendid two-story homes were put up and sold to middle-upper-class families. Speculators made tremendous profits and over-built this whole section with luxury homes."

With the influx of the upper-class, and the formation of the fashionable "Stuyvesant Heights" section and its mansions of the wealthy, came servants. And the servants needed places to live. They formed the first Negro community in the Bedford area, over toward the east where Fulton Street slums were marching out slowly but persistently from Flatbush Avenue and downtown Brooklyn.

The collapse of Stuyvesant Heights society came during the early 1920's when prices soared, and then, with the Depression, many of the lovely brownstones became too much for their original owners to maintain. They moved out and the prices dropped until the houses were within reach of Negro families. And the families who couldn't make the mortgage payments on their own incomes were encouraged by brokers and the lack of any kind of zoning ordinances or regulations to subdivide the beautiful old brownstones into small apartments. Real-estate speculators jumped on this bandwagon. Bedford-Stuyvesant is the place where "blockbusting" developed into a fine art. Every time there was any possibility of stabilization, real-estate men would spur on the process of change by paying Negroes to stage brawls on street corners to frighten white residents. Nearly every day's mail contained post-cards reading, "we have a buyer for your house." Mrs. Martha Ross Leigh, whose parents settled in the neighborhood on their marriage in 1890, recalls the appearance of waves of speculators on her front porch promising "cash for your house," and urging that she "get on the gravy train." If there was a "gravy train" it ran off the tracks as far as the people who bought the houses were concerned. Brownstones purchased by speculators for $3,000 were reported to have been sold the following week to Negroes for prices as high as $20,000. The high mortgage payments were met, of course, by the rent payments of those who moved into the subdivided apartments in the old mansions. Soon Bedford-Stuyvesant began to take on the character of a Harlem suburb. Migration of Negro families along the major east-west arteries soon overwhelmed the white families, and they began moving out, especially along Fulton Street, and Gates and Myrtle Avenues.

Myrtle Avenue boasts one of the last two surviving completely elevated trains in New York City (the other is the Bronx fragment of what used to be the Third Avenue Elevated in Manhattan). The portion of the Myrtle Avenue El which runs through Bedford-Stuyvesant was constructed in 1888, and looks it. The cars which shriek intolerably over its rails all day and all night are probably the oldest in the city transit system, and the effect of the elevated on what was a depressing street to begin with, inspired Henry Miller to write of Myrtle Avenue:

Down this street no saint ever walked (else it would have crumbled), down this street no miracle ever passed, nor any poet, nor any species of human genius, nor did any flower ever grow there, nor did the sun strike it squarely, nor did the rain ever wash it. For the genuine Inferno which I had to postpone for 20 years, I give you Myrtle Avenue, one of the innumerable bridlepaths ridden by iron monsters which lead to the heart of America's emptiness. . . . It is a street not of sorrow, for sorrow would be human and recognizable, but of sheer emptiness: it is emptier than the most extinct volcano, emptier than a vacuum, emptier than the word God in the mouth of an unbeliever.

Myrtle Avenue is not the only Bedford-Stuyvesant block blighted by elevateds, however. It is an indication of the neglect of the entire area that there are three elevated lines within, or on the borders of this slum; that the Long Island Rail Road is elevated here, and that there are also three subways which serve it. Actually, the one real advantage that may be found in Bedford-Stuyvesant living is the availability of cheap public transportation.

As still more Negroes came, from the South and from Harlem as well, the rest of Bedford-Stuyvesant lost its suburban characteristics. It was 52 percent nonwhite in 1950, and the white churches which had held on gamely for upwards of twenty years began to give up and get out. Ten years later the percentage of Negroes and Puerto Ricans was conservatively figured at 83. And this took in the white Pratt Institute enclave. As early as 1940 the area had been blighted by subhuman slums. In 1952, after a fire killed a family of seven in a dismal cellar apartment, a grand jury took a look at Bedford-Stuyvesant. It reported "occupancy of dark, damp and filthy cellars that defy description, and families of six, and more, cooking, eating and sleeping in one room, lacking proper toilet and bathing facilities." Little was done until two years ago when Borough President Abe Stark discovered these "appalling" living conditions and "buildings . . . unfit for human habitation."

Stark's pressure on the Buildings Department did manage to get Bedford-Stuyvesant slumlords some of the

111

attention that their Harlem counterparts had been receiving. And in an area where garbage collection is no small matter the Department of Sanitation scheduled garbage pickups six days a week.

But even before Bedford-Stuyvesant caught the attention of city authorities it had begun to come into its own in Negro America. Bedford-Stuyvesant people took great pride in the fact that singer Lena Horne was born there, and when, in 1947, the Brooklyn Dodgers became the first major league ball club to give a Negro a chance, thousands of Bedford-Stuyvesant residents made daily and nightly treks in the summer to nearby Ebbets Field, just south of Bedford-Stuyvesant, to cheer Jackie Robinson.

The forties also saw the emergence of the area politically and socially. Although Harlemites might still slight Brooklyn Negroes by saying "when a colored man can't afford to live in Harlem any longer, he moves to Bedford-Stuyvesant," the truth was that prices in both areas by then were on a par, and a new social awareness was in the making in the minds of Bedford-Stuyvesant Negroes. Today, Bedford-Stuyvesant is still a kind of "Second City" to Harlem, and Harlemites still boast of a "cultural lag" in the area's residents; yet the ties that link the two range even deeper than the IND subway which takes thirty-one minutes to make the run from 125th Street and St. Nicholas Avenue in Harlem to Fulton Street and Nostrand Avenue in Bedford-Stuyvesant. The train that makes the trip, traveling down the length of Manhattan and under the East River and the civic center of Brooklyn, is celebrated in the jazz classic, "Take the A Train."

Quite a few people did take the A train, too: Bedford-Stuyvesant people traveling up to Harlem for a night on the town, and businessmen who had found profit in catering to Negro needs—especially credit—making the trip in the other direction to open new markets. With the latter, unfortunately, came the policy bankers and the dope pushers, also intent on new markets. At present, there are some very nice shops in Bedford-Stuyvesant, but if a woman is looking for something really stylish she goes to Harlem. If a man is looking for something a little more exciting, and possibly a little more illegal, than a movie or a drink in a fairly good nightclub, he will probably go over to Harlem to find it. That isn't to imply that there aren't brothels and narcotics shooting galleries in Bedford-Stuyvesant. There are, and some are as degrading as anything Harlem has to offer. But none are as sophisticated or really as exciting as the first-class places in the Negro capital of the world.

The fact that Bedford-Stuyvesant was less exciting, and therefore a little more peaceful, had a corresponding effect in the attraction to Bedford-Stuyvesant of Negroes rising into the middle classes and looking to settle down. A few years ago, in answer to a particularly one-sided series of articles, "Inside the Bedford-Stuyvesant Jungle" in the now-defunct New York *Mirror*, Richard A. Brennan, chairman of the board of the Brevoort Savings Bank at Fulton and Nostrand, wrote:

"And so the larger part of Bedford-Stuyvesant was transformed, made far more populous, but became as stable a community as any in the city for the purchasers were serious, self-respecting socially adequate families. They were proud to be in possession of sound property in a central area accessible to cheap public transportation. It follows that they were and are zealous in taking care of their purchases. From the banking standpoint I gladly assert that their record of living up to their contractual obligations is as good as that of any."

Reinforcing this are the hundred-odd "block associations" which compete in the Neighborhood Council's annual Christmas contest for the best seasonal decorations, and which organize, from time to time, clean-up drives on their own blocks and maintain signs in every third or fourth front yard urging cleanliness in appearance, and in language as well.

Primarily because Bedford-Stuyvesant was once a suburb there is a lot more greenery along everything but the major arteries than in Harlem. The houses into which Negro families are crammed sometimes boast front and back yards. The streets they face are wider and not as confining as those of Harlem, and the houses are not as tall, three or four stories at most. Most of them lack the ready access to the roofs provided in Harlem tenements. This was one of the few things that Brooklyn police had reason to be grateful for during the rioting in Bedford-Stuyvesant.

On the other hand, passable as the exteriors of most of the houses might be, the interiors of many are awful. Kenny Rice, coordinator of the Rent Strike Committee of the area Congress of Racial Equality, says he has tenants of 225 buildings participating in rent strikes: i.e., withholding their rents until the buildings are fixed up. Rice says most of these houses "are in terrible condition, rat infested. There are holes in the ceilings, roofs are falling in, in some cases so are floors. . . . The landlord in most cases never visits these houses. Nine and a half times out of ten he is white. In some instances we have landlords that haven't gotten a cent in rent for months, and still they never come around."

114

Even today, real-estate brokers on Fulton Street are proclaiming windowcard advertisements of tenements for sale, "no services to tenants" required.

And then there are the housing projects, nine of them at present, including the Fort Greene development which, with 13,210 registered occupants, is larger by 5,000 than its nearest competitor in size, Marcy Houses. The nine projects, the New York Housing Authority reports, hold an estimated 47,100 residents who pay rent of approximately $13.63 per room. The Authority figures show a total construction cost of $122,616,000 for the nine projects. In the works, at present, are four more projects for 5,020 residents at a cost of $28,257,000.

But the neatly classified statistics hardly reflect the real conditions in many of these projects. Reporter Rubenstein calls them the real breeding places of the fighting gangs that swarm over the area. The Youth Board lists twenty-two fighting gangs in Bedford-Stuyvesant, with a conservative membership estimate of 1,000. The projects, Rubenstein says, have become headquarters and refuges for the gangs, a handy place to meet before going out on marauding raids, and an even handier place to return to for sanctuary from other organized gangs. The gangs, he says, are responsible for an air of lawlessness among all the youths of Bedford-Stuyvesant and a resulting lack of interest, an "oh, the hell with it" attitude among their elders. "The city tries to keep these projects in good condition, but the kids make it impossible. They break windows, write on walls, turn them into slop houses. The city tried everything, threw in all kinds of help, but you can't keep up with these kids."

But it's not only the kids. Bedford-Stuyvesant has everything wrong with it that you might expect from any ghetto, only in most cases it has it worse. The police estimate that the homicide rate in Bedford-Stuyvesant is six times that of the city as a whole, and there are about eight times as many arrests for narcotics violations there. Average family income in the area is estimated at a little more than $4,000 per year. The male unemployment rate, as reported by the Bureau of Labor Statistics in a study of neighborhoods, ranged as high as 17.3 percent, compared to a city average of 5.0 percent.

Louis Hennigan, director of the City Labor Department office on Fulton Street, estimates the Bedford-Stuyvesant unemployment average at 12 percent, at least double the national rate. "The people who come in here about 90 percent of the time are unemployed now, and always will be unemployable. They are the low men on the totem pole." Automation, which has been taking such a toll in Harlem, is also the biggest problem in the Bedford-Stuyvesant labor picture. Brooklyn factories are switching over to automation in their packing, shipping, and mailing operations, traditional factory employments in which Negroes dominated. "There never has been any long-term employment for these people," Hennigan says. "Only three-, four-or five-month jobs. I imagine if some of them got long-time work they would feel uneasy.

"The greatest lag comes across in education, formal and informal. It seems to me there is a philosophy that no matter how much you apply yourself and go to school, there is no use doing it because you're still Negro, and there's no use trying to get above the mob." Adding to the problem is insufficient education displayed by the Southern Negroes, still immigrating into the ghetto in sizable numbers. "Two out of three of the people who walk in here come from the South," Hennigan says. "And so recently

116

that not only do we have to find something for them, but we have to give them directions on how to get there." He cites two examples of what he is up against:

"Two products of a Southern Negro college came in. Both had bachelors degrees in mechanical arts. I thought this would be a snap. Big companies are crying for qualified Negro college graduates. I sent them down to the telephone company. They gave them a basic test—just a formality—and these two flunked. They answered eight questions out of fifty. Questions on stuff we got in the eighth grade. These guys have college degrees and they didn't know how to spell college."

Hennigan's other example is a girl who said she was "desperate" for any kind of a job. An appointment was set up for her at the United States Pavilion at the World's Fair, but the girl failed to keep it. "I couldn't go out there that day," she said later, "it was raining."

"We've had about 7,000 registrants here," Hennigan reports. "We've placed about 1,000 of them. It may not sound like much to you, but we think it's wonderful." The labor official has been in charge of the Fulton Street branch ever since a year ago when the city recognized the practicality of putting a labor office where the unemployment was. A former trade union official, Hennigan said that in his lifetime he had seen a lot, but that Bedford-Stuyvesant shocked him. "Everything goes on here. Numbers, narcotics, I see them here right in front of my eyes. You should see some of the things I see."

Aside from the regular employment office, the city has recently set up a block away, an office of Job Opportunities in Neighborhoods, or JOIN. The office was set up as part of the agreement ending a Negro employment protest on a city construction project, the Downstate Medical Center in Brooklyn. JOIN is designed to get Negroes into industrial training programs and craft unions, and there is friction between its staff and that of the staff of the other city employment office. The newcomers are considered visionaries and ivory-tower planners, and they, in turn, consider the labor department people as hack social workers. In Bedford-Stuyvesant, the JOIN office director, Dr. Boris von Arnold, reports notable success in developing a program with a local automobile agency garage. Nonetheless, he said, in any typical two-month period, his office interviews 360 applicants; refers 91 for job interviews, and places 38.

What caused the ghetto that is Bedford-Stuyvesant today? This is one of the few things that both church and political leaders agree on. It was the panic of the white community in moving away during the late 30's, 40's, and early 50's that turned Bedford Corners and Stuyvesant Heights from an almost all white area into a Negro slum. As blocks went Negro, schools were swallowed up. Teachers with seniority began to ask transfers to Flatbush and elsewhere where they felt they could, in the words of one, "teach, not rule" classes. Today Bedford-Stuyvesant schools are manned largely by substitute teachers. In some schools up to 60 percent of the staff are substitutes.

The increase in crime, bad teaching, and worsening of the neighborhoods had one notable effect. Negroes who had come to Bedford-Stuyvesant in the first wave of migration to get away from the horror that Harlem was becoming, found themselves no better off, and began looking for other places to go. Some made short-term jumps into Crown Heights, Williamsburg, East New York, and Brownsville, and caused the same cycle to begin again as white home owners put their houses up for sale to additional Negroes and went out to Long Island where, for the time being, it was "safe."

Other Bedford-Stuyvesant Negroes made long jumps, to South Jamaica and Corona in Queens, and these areas began to be considered little ghettos, too. Behind the migrants, however, Bedford-Stuyvesant did not lack replacements. The Bureau of Labor Statistics study showed that in the high-unemployment tracts in Bedford-Stuyvesant the average household size was 3.4 persons, compared with 2.9 for the city as a whole. And these kids were growing up.

With the increase in Negro density in Bedford-Stuyvesant came the expected political maneuvering. So far, the white community in Brooklyn, by dint of a neat bit of gerrymandering, has managed to carve Bedford-Stuyvesant up and divide it among three congressional districts, so the Bedford-Stuyvesant Negro has no Adam Clayton Powell to match Harlem. As the area first started to "turn," the Negro community was juggled between two Assembly districts in an effort to keep their representation white, but that soon proved a losing cause, and eventually, instead of gerrymandering Negroes out of the district, political leaders conceded the Assembly seat to them— Bertram Baker has represented the sixth Assembly district for more than sixteen years—and devoted their efforts to attempting to gerrymander Negroes into the sixth, thus hoping to keep the parent seventeenth district white. When Bedford-Stuyvesant began to spread rapidly, the seventeenth, by then one of the most irregular political districts ever created—roughly it surrounds the sixth on the north, east, and south in a crazy kind of crescent— went along with it, and now it, too, is represented by a Negro, Tom Jones.

Paralleling the growth of political organizations was that of civic ones. The Brooklyn branch of the NAACP is in Bedford-Stuyvesant, and is one of the stronger chapters.

There is also a headquarters of the United African Nationalists on Fulton Street, but as yet there is no Black Muslim mosque.

Nonetheless, because Harlem is considered the big league, the natural leaders of Bedford-Stuyvesant—good and bad—have a tendency to gravitate there. The lack of such leadership—good and bad—has hurt Bedford-Stuyvesant materially. As an example, the $117 million-program for HARYOU came into being on July 1, but it wasn't until July 23, almost as an afterthought, that Bedford-Stuyvesant—where there are more Negroes—was remembered, and Mayor Robert Wagner signed a contract for a minuscule $223,000 for a Bedford-Stuyvesant social project to be called "Youth in Action, Inc."

By the late 50's, even though Bedford-Stuyvesant had lost its suburban characteristics, its leaders, primarily churchmen, still clung to the premise that the Brooklyn ghetto was not another Harlem, that there had never been any serious clashes between the Negro community and the whites it was displacing. The Reverend Gardner Taylor, minister of the Concord Baptist Church, head of the Brooklyn Protestant Council, and a former member of the Board of Education, noted in 1958 that Bedford-Stuyvesant "has never been whipped up to a froth."

Perhaps not, but just two years later Dr. Taylor, whose congregation of 10,000 is one of the largest in the nation, was warning that:

"The least spark can ignite this community. I've told Police Commissioner [Stephen P.] Kennedy that unless the community and the police can get together here and do the right thing, we're going to have a big explosion."

One thing which had whipped up sentiment to this degree, in this short a period, was an incident which received scant publicity, but which is still talked about in Bedford-Stuyvesant. A twenty-four-year-old sandblaster named Al Garrett was having a few drinks on a warm Friday night in April, 1959, and was arrested for disorderly conduct. He was taken to the 79th Precinct stationhouse at Gates and Throop Avenues and deposited in a back room there. A few minutes later the arresting officer went to question him.

According to the report of the officer, Garrett went berserk. He is said to have attacked the patrolman with a chair and knocked him to the floor. The officer pulled his gun and fired once, and Garrett, who had never been arrested before, died two weeks later in Kings County Hospital. A grand jury cleared the officer, but its "no-true-bill" failed to quiet feelings in Bedford-Stuyvesant. "As a layman," said R. Risley Dent, Jr., Brooklyn NAACP president at that time, "I wonder how in the hell they have to shoot someone in a police station." Protests were made to the offices of the governor, the mayor, the Department of Justice, and the office of the district attorney, where they were promptly filed.

But they were also filed in the collective mind of the Bedford-Stuyvesant community, and in the following year crowds reacted quickly when word spread that a stray bullet—fired by policemen chasing two burglary suspects—had killed a fourteen-year-old delivery boy on Franklin Avenue near Fulton Street. It took fifty TPF men to hold back the crowd of more than five hundred furious residents who descended on the corner to protest. "The police said they shot away from the crowd [during the chase of the bandits]," Dr. Taylor said later. "But the rumor has spread around here that the police shot into the crowd, the way they did in South Africa." Despite the shouts from the

121

near mob that came to Franklin and Fulton that "white cops are shooting down colored boys," the incident never got out of hand.

Yet some Bedford-Stuyvesant residents took their revenge later in the month by attacking a patrolman who was escorting a prisoner along Fulton Street. The prisoner called for help, the crowd moved in, and the man got away. It was an ominous warning. Those two incidents proved that Bedford-Stuyvesant could raise a mob if it wanted to. Still to be proved was whether the community could achieve its means by other, less frightening methods.

For that, Bedford-Stuyvesant had to wait three more years until the summer of 1963 when an area minister, Dr. Sandy Ray, president of the 400,000-member Empire State Baptist Convention, led equal-employment demonstrations at Downstate Medical Center. The demonstrations, through the spring and summer, resulted in the establishment of JOIN, and more important, in the first dent in the lily-white front of craft unions. Even Harlem had to take notice. Another significant—but overlooked—result of the Downstate picketing was the transfer of a Brooklyn police inspector after Dr. Taylor complained of his "intemperate and uncouth" manner toward pickets after their arrest.

Later, when a police officer suggested that the riots the following year were a direct result of the spirit of the Downstate demonstrations, Dr. Ray was flattered. "I would feel rather proud if it were true," he said. "I don't think it is. We were trying to build the kind of climate that would encourage the discontent of Negroes, not toward violence, but toward wanting to do something about it [discrimination]. I don't advocate violence because I don't think it can achieve anything. But with organized demonstrations and corresponding preparations, we can achieve our goals.

"I think the leaders have the responsibility to encourage discontent among the disadvantaged, and a leader who doesn't, doesn't fulfill his responsibility. I think we should point up negligence and injustices of the community. I think a few are corrected by both protests and demonstrations."

If it was protests and demonstrations that Dr. Ray wanted, it was both that he got. Brooklyn Negroes had had a taste of leadership in the civil rights fight, and they wanted more. One Brooklyn Negro leader was particularly active. He was the Reverend Milton Galamison, of the Shiloh Baptist Church, who formulated the Citywide Committee for Integrated Schools and pointed up the real discrimination by neighborhood patterns of New York public schools.

Galamison called for a citywide school boycott in February, and then found himself a civil rights leader of national prominence when the boycott idea caught on and drew support from NAACP and the other more conservative civil rights organizations. National leader Bayard Rustin, the man who organized the March on Washington, came over to help.

Then the city authorities took notice. New York State aid to city schools is worked out over average attendance figures, and even a one-day boycott, thanks to the complicated formulas involved, could materially reduce school aid allotments. (It didn't, a loophole was worked out.) Galamison was denounced in educational circles and by the city, which was not above citing, through its press spokesmen, the attendance at a private school of the minister's own son. With it all, the boycott was a considerable success. The Board of Education itself figured nonattendance at approximately 464,000 pupils, or 44.8 percent of its students.

Galamison was so pleased that he called another boycott, disregarding the advice of the other civil rights groups. Bayard Rustin dealt himself out this time, as did the NAACP and the other groups which had backed the first boycott, including national CORE, but not local CORE. Nonetheless, a boycott is a boycott, and 268,024 pupils, or 26.1 percent of the students, stayed out. The Board of Education chairman, James B. Donovan, noted for his role in the exchange of Communist and American prisoners, said the second boycott fizzled. Galamison called it a success, but he made no secret of his irritation with the civil rights fighters who had deserted him, and later, when the Brooklyn chapter of CORE, one of his few supporters, came up with a plan which shocked even the strongest civil rights supporters, Galamison went right along.

The plan of Brooklyn CORE was especially frightening to a city like New York. It was a civil rights protest, the like of which had never been imagined: a stall-in planned for the first day of the World's Fair.

New York roads are crowded enough, and nobody needed pictures drawn to visualize what would happen if cars were deliberately stalled on throughways and parkways choked with fairgoers. There would be chaos and the seeds of disaster in the blocking of emergency vehicles. (The week before the World's Fair opening, without even a deliberate attempt, there was a mixup in parking lot arrangements at neighboring Shea Stadium and roads were clogged for upwards of two hours.)

The wave of revulsion that swept through the city for this plan encompassed even the national CORE organization, which called in Brooklyn leaders and tried to get them to change their minds. When this failed, the Brooklyn chapter was suspended.

The stall-in failed. Brooklyn CORE officials owned no more than half a dozen cars, and the support they had hoped to come from the South never materialized. A few subway trains were delayed by really determined civil rights militants, but, on the whole, there was little interference with access to the fair and the demonstrations that national CORE Director James B. Farmer was leading there.

Brooklyn CORE and Dr. Galamison, finding themselves without effect, retired to the background and remained there even during the organization of the Macabees, a development which probably did more than anything else to spread bad feeling between the Negro community of Bedford-Stuyvesant and the Jewish community of Crown Heights. The Maccabees, named after the ancient warriors who protected Jews in pre-Christian days, were organized after an attack by an estimated fifty Negro youths on young Hasidic Jewish children at the United Lubavitcher Yeshivoth, at 1352 Bedford Avenue, one of the last vestiges of the Jewish community north of Eastern Parkway in what used to be Crown Heights.

The youthful rabbi of the Yeshiva, Samuel Schrage, organized his Macabees to "reinforce" what he called lax police protection at night in the Crown Heights area. The idea, and the resulting annoyance of the Police Department, drew widespread publicity—writeups in all New York City newspapers, and a feature story in the *Saturday Evening Post*. The implication that Crown Heights needed the extra protection because of the influx of Negro criminals from Bedford-Stuyvesant was clear, and it infuriated the political leadership of the Negro community. It did not, however, seem to antagonize, quite as much, the religious leaders of Bedford-Stuyvesant. There were twenty Negroes in the Maccabees, residents of Crown Heights who agreed with Rabbi Schrage on the need for additional protection, and despite police denunciation of "vigilante" organizations, the Maccabees even drew a modified endorsement from the Negro Ministers Movement of Brooklyn and Long Island.

But Maccabees or no Maccabees, on May 30, at 990 Montgomery Street, three blocks from their Albany Avenue headquarters, a white thirty-eight-year-old schoolteacher was raped and stabbed to death at night by a man, believed to have been a Negro, who had followed her into the elevator of her apartment building.

Through this, there was silence from Galamison and the Brooklyn CORE leaders, who appeared to have been plunged into typographical oblivion by the failure of the stall-in—read out of the civil rights movement as it were. The feeling must have rankled.

So when James Powell was shot and killed and the Harlem rioting began, Brooklyn CORE waited cautiously several days to see what was developing. It came into the picture by announcing a rally to denounce police brutality, both in the Powell shooting and the ensuing riots.

7

Tuesday, July 21

It began in Brooklyn on the morning of Tuesday, July 21, but Bedford-Stuyvesant had been preparing for it all day Monday, even if nobody else had. The *New York Times* was out that day with an editorial which seemed to say the riots were behind us: "Now the task before the city's responsible leadership—including the leaders of all major population groups—is to try to repair the political and other damage that has been done."

In Bedford-Stuyvesant, that "political and other damage" was just beginning. The Brooklyn branch of CORE, which has its store-front office nine blocks north of Fulton Street, on Nostrand, was planning its first rally to protest the Powell slaying. Also to be protested was police "brutality" to the Harlem rioters.

This was not quite as foolhardy as it may sound. The July heat had all Brooklyn on edge. Just the previous Saturday night, while riots were tearing apart Harlem, a bitter racial battle had broken out between Negroes and Puerto Ricans in Brownsville. Five men and a boy were shot, a youth was hit with acid, and two policemen were slightly hurt. Six were arrested on weapons charges.

What worried the CORE leaders was the lack of contact with youths in the fifteen- to twenty-five-year age group. CORE hoped that it could, through a strong, but nonviolent, protest, reach those youths to channel the rising dissatisfactions into some kind of a peaceful protest.

The CORE membership meeting broke up after midnight Monday with a march down Nostrand Avenue to Fulton Street. About thirty-five people paraded, singing. Notably, almost half were white. By the time they reached Nostrand they had picked up support. It was a hot night, and men spilled out of bars and into the streets to follow them. The group paused at Nostrand and Fulton and blocked traffic, but, in the words of Inspector Clerke, "they hadn't drummed up enough of a crowd, so they took a march, went by the bars a few times so that they would have the right clientele."

Gilbert Banks of CORE put it differently. CORE had decided to march around the four-square-block area to block the traffic at four main intersections before it spoke to the crowds it had collected. "The purpose of tying up traffic was to show the power structure we could tie up most of their major arteries if we chose to do so. For five years we have seen Negroes beaten. We feel it is time for whitey to share what we were suffering."

How whitey would be made to suffer in the tying up of traffic at 1 A.M. in a Negro area was not spelled out.

When the marchers finally returned to Nostrand and Fulton, CORE took over the traditional northeast corner and began its rally. As speaker followed speaker, the temperature of the exhortations rose. One of the last speakers threatened a citywide stall-in, making what the *New*

York Times' Robert McG. Thomas, the only reporter there at the time, described as inflammatory remarks.

Six policemen guarded the intersection. Police had decided to be as permissive as possible and to remain as inconspicuous as they could, to forestall charges that their very presence stirred up trouble. But the crowd grew restless and surly. CORE said that one man—a Negro who called himself an off-duty policeman, heckled the speakers, and, as CORE explained later, he "became a target for the masses." The crowds near the podium, they said, no longer paid attention to the man on the stand, but became emotional over this man's taunts.

With the growing unrest, police sent for reinforcements. A detail of twenty men appeared on the corner, and more were sent for, but their presence was—as the department had feared—inciting. Negro cops among them became the real focus of tensions. "People were shaking their fists at them and calling them Uncle Toms," Thomas reported later. "Negro women were directing sexual insults at the white policemen."

The CORE speaker was still talking, but nobody listened. In the crowd the chant of "go, go, go, go," arose. From elsewhere came the counterpoint, "killer cops must go." The chants were timed so that the word "go" in each sounded simultaneously as a beat. Still the police detail held back. The officer in charge of that detail was Captain Irving Levitan, and later the CORE leaders said that he did a "remarkable" job in holding the crowds—and his men—in check. This, of course, in the face of increasing bitterness, both from the speaker's stand and from the sidewalks. "Let's get the Jews before this is over," somebody yelled from the safety of a throng of people.

By this time at least a thousand people swarmed at the

129

corner. CORE sensed the pressing danger. The final speaker tried to send the crowds home, but he might as well have saved his breath. "They had a pretty good sized mob at one in the morning, and those people don't go home till four [after the bars close] and they had three hours on their hands," Inspector Clerke said.

The mob stirred restlessly toward the police. The CORE members asked the captain to pull his men out "so the people would not have anything to be infuriated by." The police could hardly do that: To retreat before a gathering crowd meant only disaster. CORE continued to urge the mob to leave. Another rally was promised for that night. This had no effect.

The first bottles came. They arced over the heads of the crowd and smashed at the feet of the police. The officers fingered their clubs nervously, and the CORE members, by prearrangement, locked hands and surrounded the officers. CORE was trying, Banks explained later, to impress the crowds "that there would be as little retaliation as possible."

At that instant Captain Levitan's reinforcements screeched onto the corner, brakes and sirens screaming. Bottles flew all over, most aimed at the heads of the cops.

And that was it. Police charged the crowds, nightsticks poised.

CORE later charged that the officers swung "indiscriminately," but at that point, at Nostrand and Fulton, the cops had valid cause to believe that every person they could get to was an enemy.

They were wrong, of course, and more than one innocent victim wound up in the middle. Reporter Thomas said he saw "one innocent kid hit by a cop on Fulton. He had parked his car, and had gotten into a doorway, and they were chasing somebody else into the same doorway. They beat this kid, hit him all over the body."

The police conduct during the riot situation has been generally praised. CORE officials themselves stated that the police acted with restraint and some judgment. Nonetheless, incidents of the kind reported by Thomas had happened in Harlem, and were going to happen in Bedford-Stuyvesant for the next three days. A bottle would fly, a cop would lunge. A group of people would run. In the darkness the police, chasing full tilt, would swing out around them with their nightsticks. "Sure we make mistakes," Police Commissioner Michael Murphy said later. "You do in any war." He was not saying it in apology either. In both Bedford-Stuyvesant and Harlem, Murphy thinks his men did a fine job in keeping the bloodshed down. From personal observation, the authors agree.

If there were innocent victims in the mob, there were many times more innocent victims of the mob. One was Mrs. Anna Kelter, a sixty-seven-year-old woman who lived upstairs from the grocery store she'd operated at Nostrand and Atlantic for thirty-five years. Mrs. Kelter didn't know about any demonstration. All she knew was that she had heard the glass break and had hurried downstairs to find her corner gone mad and people she had never seen before ransacking her store.

"They took a barrel in the street and pushed it through the window," she told *Journal-American* reporter Frank Borsky. "I'm here thirty-five years and nobody bothered me. They would say, 'go to Mom Kelter's store.' They love me. All of a sudden this happens. They hug and kiss me. My son-in-law and me, that's all that's here."

The most seriously hurt innocent that night, however,

was a young Negro woman who was walking home after visiting friends. She stepped onto Fulton Street and was hit by a chunk of debris.

Adding to the danger for nonparticipants in Bedford-Stuyvesant is the fact that, unlike Harlem, the Brooklyn ghetto is considered relatively safe for Negroes out at night—even for Negro women. "I feel better walking down Nostrand Avenue at night than I would feel on Fifth Avenue," said Rita Phillips, a City College student who is a volunteer CORE worker.

Many Brooklynites, especially on this first night, had not the faintest idea that violence was stalking their normally peaceful streets. Homebound night workers emerged from the subways onto Fulton Street to find themselves in the middle of a war. Some scuttled home; others stayed around to watch, and sooner or later invariably became caught up in one part or another of the mob. On the other hand, there were desertions from the mob. Some people, even in the forefront of the crowds baiting the police or running from store to store suddenly looked at watches, and then disappeared. Others left without a sign, as if suddenly they had had enough. They would turn on their heels and walk away, presumably to their homes.

Not all the violence lacked purpose, even that night. A police car belonging to the precinct Youth Squad was parked at Nostrand, a block south of Fulton, and even though it was an unmarked car, it apparently was well enough known. As police surged up from Nostrand to chase back one band of marauders, somebody behind them deliberately smashed the closed window of the car and tossed in a Molotov cocktail. By the time police got back, the car was burning furiously. It was a total loss.

Police say that on Monday night and early Tuesday

morning no shots were fired in Bedford-Stuyvesant, and reporters who were there heard none. Nonetheless, the next day a woman brought a bullet into CORE headquarters. She said that early in the morning, in the midst of a skirmish, the slug came in through the open window of her Fulton Street apartment, caromed off the ceiling, and fell, spent, to the floor. "I saw cops moving and shooting in the air," CORE member Banks said.

Another CORE member, Stanley Brezenoff, who is twenty-six and white, had been at the Fulton and Nostrand rally and was going up Nostrand Street to CORE headquarters when he noticed that he was being "looked at strangely," despite the CORE button he was displaying prominently. "I don't know how to describe real fright, but it was there," Brezenoff said. When he did reach the headquarters, Brezenoff helped other CORE members set up a first-aid station which remained open—and working— during the next three nights.

Police had hopes that the closing of the bars at four o'clock in the morning would help the situation. At first, however, this only seemed to aggravate the disorders. "They would break and loot, and then it quieted down," Inspector Clerke said. "Then you'd get re-entry into the smashed stores by people who walked in and just picked up what they could." Up and down Nostrand, all along Fulton into the dawn, burglar alarms provided a high-pitched irritating accompaniment to the sounds of breaking glass and running feet, occasionally punctuated by screamed curses and the soft, unpleasant thunk of a wooden nightstick striking flesh. Still, few were hurt, and remarkably few—only twenty-two—were arrested.

At 7 A.M. it was over. Police were still getting calls, but they were sporadic. By 8 A.M. police squads guarded streets where, according to Inspector Walter Clerke, the chief officer in Bedford-Stuyvesant until Wednesday, "you would have thought nothing had happened. People walked past broken stores without so much as a look. Everybody went about his business."

On Tuesday the police, too, went about their business. CORE's promised second rally was only twelve hours away, and this time they planned to be ready for it.

They prepared on two fronts: One was purely tactical: how many men to be deployed here, there, and wherever, and with what equipment and what communications. The other front, new in recent years, was sociological. And in Captain Edward Jenkins, commanding officer of the 79th Precinct, which encompasses most of the north section of Bedford-Stuyvesant, the department had one of its best sociologists. When Captain Jenkins was given the command he brought along, for his office wall, a picture showing him with Martin Luther King.

Captain Jenkins went to work Tuesday, even as his morning shift was trying to correlate damage reports. He called the Negro leaders listed in the precinct files and set up a meeting for the afternoon, but not in the precinct house. Picture of Martin Luther King or no—he called it for neutral territory, the Bedford YMCA.

Present at the session was every V.I.P. the captain could think of. CORE was there, and so were ministerial, political, and civic personages. But it wasn't until the meeting got under way that it was brought home to Captain Jenkins that the leadership had no following among the rioters.

Sandy Ray, prominent in the Downstate demonstrations and the pastor of the Cornerstone Baptist Church, was in the chair. The precinct commander pleaded for "careful weighing" of the risks of further rioting. It was his feeling that the leadership he had assembled could do something to quiet the mob. For three hours the leadership told him they could not. "The feeling was there was nothing we could do with the people on the street," Dr. Ray said later. "We told the captain that politicians had tried to talk to them, and that preachers had tried to talk to them. And they would say things like, 'Shut up, you have milk for your babies, we don't.' And like, 'Did whitey send you out here to talk at us, Uncle Tom?' It's pretty difficult to tell people to go home if you don't have any suggestions that will aid their grievances."

And what were their grievances? Time and time again it returned to the topic of police brutality. "The police are heavy-handed here," said Assemblyman Jones. "You feel like a fool telling people not to protest in the face of this kind of treatment."

Dr. Galamison was at that meeting, too. He asked Captain Jenkins what could be done about suspending Lieutenant Gilligan and setting up a civilian review board—matters far above the authority of a Brooklyn precinct captain. "There is a place for peaceful mediation," Galamison pointed out, "but the word *mediation* implies that you have something to mediate with. And if there are no demands which have been met, that is, in terms of the things for which the people were asking . . . then it's unfair to ask the people to cease from their disorder."

The meeting broke up with adoption of a resolution which solved nothing but which nobody could quarrel with. "Violence and disorders do not occur in a vacuum. In dealing with riots and disorder, we are dealing with symptoms rather than causes. Therefore the basic evils from which the community suffers must be corrected, because the people can no longer be restrained."

Later, when several of the leaders were asked what

they had done after the meeting, they said they had gone right home.

The police went ahead with their plans, but they—and Bedford-Stuyvesant, too, were watching out for the same thing. Mayor Robert F. Wagner, en route to Geneva for a labor conference, had turned around and was coming home. Up till now the crisis had been handled by his City Council president, Paul Screvane, who had kept the transatlantic cables humming with repeated pleas to the mayor to return. And the mayor was returning.

The civil rights groups were hoping that Wagner would capitulate to their demands for a civilian review board. Police were hoping for a tough stand.

Mayor Wagner had two choices: He could give the civil rights groups the civilian review board, which had become the symbol of the crisis, and look for a new police commissioner—or he could back Murphy and look for more trouble. After a day of waiting for the mayor to return and make that decision, the people of New York were told they would have to wait yet another day. The mayor, back in New York and ducking the civil rights leaders in favor of conferences with his aides, said he would go on television Wednesday evening.

Among those not present at the Gracie Mansion sessions was Police Inspector Clerke. Inspector Clerke had Tuesday night to worry about. He and his deputy, Dominic Hallinan, worked in and out of their Bushwick headquarters all day, while over across the river, some other people were working, too.

The Harlem Defense Council had its printers going, and conflicting reports on the planning over there sifted into Brooklyn Patrol North headquarters all day. First report was that trouble would not start until after 10:30 P.M., after the 8:30 CORE rally had dispersed. The second report was that trouble would start before the rally, at 7:30. Finally it was decided to dispatch Hallinan and thirty men to the corner of Nostrand and Fulton, and to keep twenty men in reserve away from the corner, but immediately available. A decision was also made about gunfire, with regard to warning shots.

The matter-of-fact attitude that Inspector Clerke had noted around the crossroads of Nostrand and Fulton in Bedford-Stuyvesant continued only through the daylight hours. When the sun set and darkness approached, so did tension. Two white men, strangers to each other, met in the early dusk on Nostrand above Fulton. They exchanged worried smiles. "I'm in insurance," one said. "You'd better get out of here like I am, no matter what you're in," the other retorted.

At CORE's store headquarters, above a barber shop, the atmosphere was unusually strained. A reporter there in the early evening was treated courteously and talked to, although there was no real communication. Even CORE didn't know which way it would jump, and it wouldn't know until after its executives met.

The meeting did not take long. CORE had found out what kind of fire it had played with the previous night. Oliver Leeds, the membership chairman, emerged to say that Brooklyn CORE, instead of holding its own demonstration on the corner of Nostrand and Fulton, where several hundred people were already waiting, would instead participate in civil rights demonstrations at the governor's office and City Hall in Manhattan. (Actually, the Manhattan demonstrations that night turned out to be at Police Headquarters.) "It is Brooklyn CORE's feeling that rallies and demonstrations however peaceful in the Bedford-Stuyvesant area could get out of hand," Leeds said. "Elements we could not control could seize the lead and do something we would not want." The CORE members went up Nostrand and Fulton only long enough to post signs calling on residents to "protest police brutality. Demonstrate tonight at City Hall." Then they headed for Manhattan.

Left there, in the descending twilight were upwards of five hundred people. The CORE signs were barely noticed; within a few minutes they had vanished. People had come to Bedford-Stuyvesant to watch a demonstration, and they were going to see one. The vacuum left when CORE pulled out was quickly filled by a black nationalist speaker. Various black nationalist groups had put speakers on this corner several nights a week for five years, and never had they had an audience like this. In fact, according to the cop on the beat, Patrolman Harold Lowe, a Negro officer, "they never attracted any crowds at all. They had two to four people looking on, they'd think they had something. And nobody ever listened to what they had to say."

This night, hundreds on the four corners were waiting to listen to "what they had to say" and the militant black nationalists were not about to disappoint them. The nationalist came onto the northeast corner and set up a podium, on which was tacked a "Buy Black" sign, mounted it, and began his harangue. Within minutes, most of the five hundred people at the intersection were heading for his corner. They were a responsive crowd, too, cheering as the speaker threw out such comments as "No white man has ever done anything for us." As he spoke, the policemen, white and Negro, seven and eight to each corner, began fingering their clubs. They were wearing soft caps, not helmets, at that time, and there were those in the crowds who were sizing them up. Out of the middle of the throng surrounding the speaker came young boys and girls carrying stacks of the "Gilligan Wanted for Murder" poster. One youth offered one of the posters to a white reporter, the only white reporter on the corner at the moment. The reporter shook his head and grinned nervously. "I've seen 'em," he said.

"You'll be seeing a lot of 'em soon," the youth said curtly, and walked on handing them out.

As the crowd grew around the speaker's stand it began drifting out into the street, and there was some hindrance to traffic along Fulton, but, still, police did not move. In the next fifteen minutes, a detail of helmeted police marched in. Although the police helmets were not the first on the corners—members of the crowd had thought to bring their own that night and one or two were labeled with American Legion emblems—they were the first confirmation that police had been planning for extraordinary trouble. The sight of the helmets drew derisive cheers and laughter and added to the tension. Even the nationalist speaker began worrying that things were beginning to become dangerous. "I would like you to remain calm," he began suddenly after twenty minutes of denouncing the white race and urging action. The contradiction was not lost on his audience. There was laughter. "You are under the impression that by emotionalism you will impress the world, but you will not impress anybody," the man said from his "Buy Black" podium.

Finally, what police had been fearing happened. The sidewalk density had become too much and a window of a drug store on the northeast corner shattered. The crowds did not wait for the police to start after them. They fled.

In a minute the corner was nearly empty. The speaker talked on as if nothing had happened.

The police seemed uncertain. One officer walked over to the window and kicked the broken pieces of glass back against the building. Another started toward the speaker and then stopped. The speaker took no notice; he was still urging calm, and, apparently for that reason, there was no attempt to stop him. The police debated whether or not to put a guard on the broken window, but there didn't seem to be anything valuable inside it except a cardboard display. They left it alone and walked away. The crowd came back, stronger than it had been before. The speaker had no amplifying equipment, however, and by this time his voice was beginning to weaken. Besides, his message of "patience" was not what was wanted, and the crowd began to look for distractions.

Suddenly a girl broke loose from the throng and ran east on Fulton Street. She was holding something she had taken from the broken store window. Laughter followed her up the street, and then, as counterpoint, the sound of shots from a short block away. Inspector Clerke later characterized these sounds as firecrackers, but there had been occasional firecrackers before on Fulton Street, and this did not sound like firecrackers to the crowd, nor to the reporter who was there.

The greater part of the crowd did not run from what it thought was gunfire, but toward it. Many of the police on the corner followed, and more police in prowl cars, their sirens screaming, also rushed west on Fulton Street. In a minute the corner was virtually empty, except for the nationalist speaker, still on his podium, and still warning against rioting. "They'll shoot you down," he warned.

And, indeed, on this night the police had their guns out.

They were shooting primarily into the air and at rooftops, but, on occasion, to kill. Two men were shot that night. One, police said, was caught in a gang of looters at a grocery store about a block away from CORE headquarters. The police version is that the man hurled a can of vegetables at a patrolman before the officer fired. One CORE member who saw the incident swears that the man who was shot wasn't even one of the looters, that he saw the cops coming and began to run along with everybody else and was shot. "My brother got a hi-fi and a TV set from the same corner," the CORE member added.

Another man hurt early Wednesday morning was shot in the only major incident of violence reported south of Atlantic Avenue. This particular victim, police said, was taking advantage of their concentration on Fulton Street to get himself a pair of shoes from a store near Eastern Parkway. An off-duty patrolman, on his way home in civilian clothes, saw the looting, and ordered the man to come out with his hands up. Instead, the man came out with a leap toward the officer. The cop fired and the man hit the pavement with a bullet in his stomach. Police later had to send a detail racing down Nostrand Avenue to disperse a menacing group which had surrounded the policeman and his victim as they waited for an ambulance.

But earlier in the evening there were no cops that could be spared from Fulton Street. Up at least through midnight it needed every cop it could get. One of the authors of this volume—Shapiro—found himself in a perilous situation when he followed the mob making its first surge west from Nostrand on Fulton. Shots were coming from Franklin by then, and he hoped to get over there. One of the first things to go had been the street lights, and, except for the corners, there were few lights on the street. But it wasn't until he had gotten half a block over toward Bedford, right opposite the Arlington Place intersection, that the reporter realized he had put himself right in the middle of a band of looters. It isn't often that crimes are committed in the presence of reporters, and Shapiro watched incredulously while looting took place all around him. Well-dressed men and women broke out window glass and grabbed items almost indiscriminately. Then there were those who shopped for what they wanted. One man, dressed in a conservative blue suit, picked up an ash can and hurled it into the window of a five-and-ten-cent store. Then he reached in, carefully protecting his arm from the shattered glass, picked up a cheap suitcase, and started to walk off with it. Before he had taken more than a few steps, though, somebody—apparently a friend—said something to him. The man turned on his heel, walked back to the window, reached in carefully again, and brought out another suitcase which he gave to his friend, and both walked off carrying their suitcases.

Shapiro had been so engrossed in watching this that he had not noticed a group of about eight or nine young adults and boys come up behind him. When he realized they were looking at him, it was too late to make the run back to Nostrand Avenue. Instead, trying to act as if he were not afraid, as if the press card conspicuously pinned to his suit gave him some kind of immunity, he crossed to the north side of Fulton Street, angling up toward Bedford Avenue. The band of youths and young adults was right behind him. "Let's get whitey," one began, and soon there was a chant of it, rising even above the chorus of dozens of burglar alarms. Shapiro walked faster, deliberately trying to keep himself from breaking into a run—unlike Montgomery in Harlem, he wouldn't have had a chance in

142

a footrace. Meanwhile, the band behind him had swelled, and the chant was no longer "let's get whitey." It was "let's kill whitey." There was one lighted spot on the street, a theater marquee almost at Bedford Avenue. A crowd stood there, too, and he had no reason to believe its members would be any friendlier than those who were following him, but Shapiro headed for it, trembling and trying not to show it.

A youth, casually dressed, detached himself from the group underneath the marquee and began walking toward the reporter, who did not know what to expect.

What he got was the biggest favor of his life. "Let him alone," the youth yelled to the boys behind Shapiro. He walked past the reporter, who only got a fleeting glimpse of him, and was afraid to glance back for a better look. There was a crash of glass behind him, and he heard the youth yell, "hey look at that," and then the crowd behind him was off, running back away from him. Somewhat weak in the knees, Shapiro kept on, under the marquee where he was ignored by the rest of the crowd, and out onto Bedford Avenue where there was a prowl car just out of sight around the corner. Shapiro had other things to worry about that night, so he did not notice what was playing at the movie house. Later, when doing research for this volume, he checked to see what the Regent was showing. There were "Three thrill hits: *Cop Hater, The Hanging Tree,* and *When Hell Breaks Loose.*"

The youth who made a point of diverting the mob away from Shapiro was not the only Negro on the streets to offer help to a whitey. From Bedford, Shapiro continued west to Franklin, not so much to find out what the shooting was all about, but because there were more cops there and it was safer.

He had almost reached Franklin when a Negro man, sitting at the wheel of a parked car, called to him: "Let me drive your ass out of here before you get yourself killed." It was the best offer Shapiro had heard all night, but by this time he was almost up to the cops as they milled around under the overhead viaduct which marks the terminal of the Franklin Avenue shuttle to Prospect Park. He thanked the man in the car most courteously and scuttled under the viaduct. Behind him, as he went under the passenger walkway, a whisky bottle smashed on the trunk of a car.

The shots, which had first attracted the police and fire equipment over to Franklin Avenue, had stemmed from police firing at rooftops after the first Molotov cocktail of the evening had fallen at their feet. The corner was quieting down by this time, but now, shooting had broken out on Nostrand Avenue. This left Shapiro with the problem of how to get back. Traffic was somehow still coming along Fulton, in both east and west directions—a calculated tactic, Inspector Clerke said later, "to keep them [the crowds] from making a ball into the middle of the street, to keep them from gathering into a surge which would have washed us right off the street." This tactic—hard as it may have been on some of the drivers who came into the area without realizing what was going on—seems to have paid off.

The trip back to Fulton Street was comparatively uneventful. Between Bedford and Arlington, a bottle, filled with some kind of liquid, sped past within a few feet of Shapiro's head—still, it wasn't aimed at him but at a passing police car, which it also missed. On the east corner of Arlington, four cops stood close together, and Shapiro paused in the doorway of a looted dress store to get his breath. While he waited there were more shouts and shooting from Nostrand and one of those "surges of humanity" Inspector Clerke was to mention later, came pounding up the street.

The police, apparently acting under orders, began waving them through with their nightsticks. "Go on, you bastards, run," was one of the nicer remarks by the cops; another was "yipee-yi-yo-ki-yay, get along little dogies" which one cop was yelling as the crowd surged past him without interference. All this went on good-naturedly until one cop—heaven knows where he had been, perhaps chasing the guy who had thrown the bottle a few minutes before—came around the corner of Arlington Place. Apparently preoccupied, he hadn't realized anything was going on till he looked up and saw those crowds coming at him. He raised his nightstick and began flailing indiscriminately. He hit one or two of the running men without causing visible damage—they kept running—before his fellow cops could call him off.

What had set the crowds to running, it turned out, was the work of police in clearing a spot at Nostrand Avenue for the arrival of a prowl car with six thousand additional rounds of ammunition. Police normally buy their own bullets and rarely carry more than two dozen rounds at any one time. At this point in the evening, many officers were beginning to worry about running short.

Police had sent for the ammunition, though, not so much because they thought that it would be used during the night, but to ease the minds of the men that ammunition would be available if needed. As the first officers approached the prowl car to replenish their bullet supply, photographers crowded up for pictures. But police, fearing this would damage their public image, drove them away.

With the ammunition came the police mobile communications headquarters. It set up at Fulton and Nostrand, drawing power by hooking up to a power source conveniently tucked into a light pole. The police had radio, but they had no telephones. Police headquarters consisted of two pay phones. One of Inspector Clerke's headaches that night was keeping reporters from using those phones.

A reporter on a riot assignment worries more about phones than on more routine jobs. In Bedford-Stuyvesant, as elsewhere, many of the corner pay phone booths have been deliberately jammed. They take the dime, ring happily, and present the would-be caller with a dead receiver. Later, presumably, the jammer will come along with a screwdriver and unjam the phone, reaping a harvest of dimes through the coin return.

Even when a working phone was found it was dangerous. Lighted, they made fine targets. Also, a man inside one could easily have been trapped. Reporter Martin Tolchin of the *New York Times* was calling his story in on one occasion as mounted police chased a looter along Fulton Street. The looter decided to get into the phone booth, too. It didn't work out too well, but fortunately neither Tolchin nor the looter was hurt.

Because of the danger of the exposed outside phone booths, some reporters made deals with countermen at one or more of the corner luncheonettes. That worked for a short time only because the managers of the lunch stands came to the conclusion that nobody on the corners at that point was much interested in eating, and they closed.

Then a reporter found that the subway phones were working, and that solved the problem. The phones on the subway platforms were especially safe because police were guarding the stations and forbidding anyone to enter them, and, at the same time, the Transit Authority had ordered its train crews to pass up three stops in the area, and the trains were speeding past the deserted platforms carrying a number of furious passengers who hadn't gotten the word and who found themselves being carried far past their stops. Although the lack of notification was regrettable, the abandonment of the three stations was undoubtedly a wise decision. Before the step was taken, at least one Bedford-Stuyvesant resident had been hurt coming out of the subway. A young boy had unsuspectingly climbed up the subway stairs and had been hit in the head with a rock thrown at police who were chasing looters east on Fulton.

The closing of the subway stops, both in Bedford-Stuyvesant and downtown where Police Headquarters was being picketed, had inconvenienced, but not discouraged, the CORE pickets who had demonstrated, and returned, and were helping out at their first-aid station.

Oliver Leeds, the spokesman for that night, walked down to Fulton and Nostrand where he found a group of reporters and cameramen clustered together for safety, watching the mobs. Leeds looked for the signs CORE had posted about the City Hall demonstration, and then, not finding them, he said, "Well, we tried."

"What are you going to have to say about the Cossack cops tomorrow?" one reporter sardonically asked the CORE spokesman.

"It does seem," Leeds said cautiously, and in character, "that all these police are uncalled for." The reporter, who thought many more police should be called for, snorted. "What about all those stores being looted up around CORE?" he asked.

"Negroes taking revenge for years of being squeezed, penny by penny, by greedy shopkeepers," Leeds said.

"Talk about prejudice," the reporter began. The rest of his comment was unprintable.

Another onlooker with an excellent view of conditions on Fulton Street, although not from Nostrand, was George Fleary, first vice president of the Brooklyn branch of the NAACP. Fleary is a partner in a law firm located on the south side of Fulton, around the corner from Bedford. He had gone up to Nostrand earlier, just long enough to watch the mob form at the behest of the black nationalist speaker. After the window broke and the crowd surged away, he thought it was all over and went home. He was preparing for bed when his partner, Paul Gibson, called him back. Fleary parked and walked down Bedford just as a fire truck came by and stopped, "and [he said later] almost simultaneously somebody threw a bottle past them through a glass window of a store. One of the firemen came toward a group of teen-agers standing across Bedford Avenue from the broken store window, and he had his ax raised.

" 'Which one of you little bastards threw that bottle?'

" 'Nobody,' one of the kids answered. Then the fireman threw the ax down at the ground right at this kid's foot, and another fireman had to come over and take him away.

"I walked to Bedford and Fulton. Just as I turned the corner somebody fired a gun right in front of my face. Police were running into a drug store and pulling a Negro out of the doorway toward a patrol car in the street. A lot of that firing was unnecessary," added Fleary, a military police captain during World War II. He walked on to his office, and before it he found a group of teen-agers. He brought them into the office and they, and he, spent the rest of the night watching the alarms and excursions of police and looters.

Another Bedford-Stuyvesant resident with an excellent view was Mrs. Ophelia Bryant, who lives on Herkimer Street. Herkimer is the street just south of Fulton at Nostrand and at Bedford, and an obvious place for looters to seek refuge.

"It started after nine," Mrs. Bryant reported. "Somebody threw a rock in the drug store [at Herkimer and Bedford], but nobody went in at first, and they were all standing around, and then the cops came and there was a stampede. But as soon as the cops would leave they would go back and break even more windows.

"While the cops were down at Nostrand and Fulton, people would go up on Bedford and Herkimer. They started stealing, taking things like chairs and linens. I was standing outside my house looking till they came up the street. A lot of people came by with TV sets and they came up the street. And then more came by with more TV sets, and radios, beautiful chairs, red velvet things and whisky by the quart. They were selling whisky for $3 a quart, good Scotch. I think everybody on Herkimer Street was drunk.

"A crowd was coming up the street then, running, the cops behind them. We didn't know who the cops were going to shoot, and we ran in the house, then after they passed, we came out again. It must have happened that way half a dozen times."

And it kept up like that all night, not only on Herkimer Street, but north in Bedford-Stuyvesant, all the way to De Kalb Avenue and it spread east and west on Fulton Street as well.

But though the looting kept up until after dawn again, the danger of uncontrollable riot was diminishing as it grew later. Except for the one crowd which collected dangerously after the looter was shot at Eastern Parkway, the numbers of people on the streets had dropped enough that by 1:30 A.M., some police were pulled off the corners.

At about 2 A.M., when the crowds were all but gone, a few people who had not been out before, came into the streets to survey the damage. A few gathered, not menacing but curious, around a broken shop window where several white policemen were standing guard. One cop was detailed to get them back from the window, and he came over and said he was "tired of you damn niggers."

A little boy of about nine or ten, with his mother, looked the cop right in the eye. "You think you're having trouble tonight, just wait till tomorrow," he said.

8

Wednesday, July 22

Wednesday in Bedford-Stuyvesant was the day for stories.
And there were as many as there were witnesses to the
Tuesday night rioting.

At NAACP headquarters somebody mentioned the man
walking up Tompkins Avenue in the early morning, happily gnawing an uncooked ham; and the boy in a vandal-
ized shoe store trying on pair after pair of sneakers until
he found exactly the right size.

At CORE they had stories, too. Somebody had seen an
officer chasing a band of girls off a stoop where they had
been innocently watching the action. The trouble was
that the next time he told the story it was a band of old
ladies that the cop had chased. CORE had some other
stories, too, one about the store owner who came along
in the middle of a looting session, found cops chasing
kids out of his store, called off the cops, and said, "let
them have it." And there was the mother who stood look-
out for her twelve-year-old son while he stole shoes and
clothes for a back-to-school outfit.

There were stories from the streets. One was of the woman who had walked down Herkimer Street at the height of the trouble, happily sweltering under the six dresses she was wearing, dresses which she claimed to have selected carefully from the broken windows of six stores.

Police had stories, too. Two officers in a radio car had spotted an older woman on Bedford Street as she was carrying a lamp, its price tag still attached. When the woman saw the officers she shrugged and set the heavy lamp down carefully and regretfully inside the grounds of the Scottish Rite Temple.

There were stories from Big John. Big John belongs to no group and no organization, yet he and some friends were marched off more than one stoop that night by over-worked, and, according to Big John, overanxious police. "One time this cop was marching us along, and he said something we didn't catch, and my friend turned back to ask him what he'd said, and he brought that stick right down on top of my friend's head." But Big John's favorite story came from Lexington and Sumner Avenues where he watched a Negro man start an argument with a Negro cop. "The argument was the same old thing, police brutality, and all about Uncle Tom, and the black policeman didn't want to discuss it. The man jumped on him. The cop shouted stop, and when the man didn't, then he shot—only one time, and that in the air. He got the man off his back —and that was a hell of a lot better than Gilligan and Powell."

Some people had no time for stories. Merchants came to their stores to find broken glass and merchandise missing in wholesale lots. One Franklin Avenue grocery store owner estimated that he had lost between $1,500 and

$2,000 in products and cash. He interrupted his boarding-up to go around the corner to a competitor to buy a pack of cigarettes; there wasn't a pack left in his own store.

The boarding-up was urged by police, who warned all shopkeepers that more looting was to be expected. By mid-morning, Fulton, Nostrand, Bedford, and Franklin resounded to the banging of hammers.

Not every merchant took the police advice, however. One liquor store owner demonstrated his faith in the community anew each day by replacing his shattered glass window. In four days he put in four windows.

Most losses were not covered by insurance, and so were assumed directly by the merchants. Insurance companies make it exceptionally difficult, and exceptionally expensive, to get insurance in the ghetto. There is very little profit in taking high risks.

The merchants who were boarding up, and some who weren't, both Negro and white, took another precaution. They put up signs saying, "This is a black store" or "Negro-owned." A Chinese laundryman next door to CORE posted a sign saying, "This store owned by a black man" and emerged unscathed. How that "black man" would have fared if his establishment had stocked liquor instead of laundry is, however, open to question.

The vandalism on CORE's block of Nostrand Avenue was particularly heavy, a sore point with police. "All those CORE guys were sitting around on those steps watching all this going on," one cop said later. "Not one of 'em called us, not one of 'em moved to stop what they saw with their own eyes. I guess they figure law and order is something that only cops have to respect."

CORE's answer, through an official, was that to have attempted to stop the looting would have been foolhardy

—and useless—and to have called police would have branded them as finks and destroyed their chances of channeling the protest into more acceptable forms. This was not an answer calculated to appease the shopkeepers in that particular block, but these merchants had never expected more from CORE, and, besides, they had more to do on Wednesday than wonder what "these crazy kids across the street" were going to do. What they wanted to know was what the city was going to do if the rioting continued Wednesday night.

Though the merchants wouldn't have believed it, somebody was doing something—something, that is, other than sitting around waiting for Mayor Wagner to appear on television in the early evening. Brooklyn Borough President Abe Stark was doing something, and so was the Brooklyn branch of NAACP.

Abe Stark had heard about the trouble in Bedford-Stuyvesant late. A written statement put out by his office after the rioting ended says, "The first disorders in the Borough of Brooklyn occurred on the night of Tuesday, July 21st." Just what the borough president calls the epilogue to the CORE meeting of Monday, July 20th, isn't clear.

But if Stark was starting late, at least he was starting. The Brooklynite had been president of New York's City Council, and thus Mayor Wagner's number two man, until the elections of 1961, when he was rather harshly dumped and demoted to Brooklyn borough president. Relations between the two men have not been quite so cordial since that time, and, in this instance at any rate, Stark was on his own.

On Wednesday morning he met with his deputy borough president, John F. Hayes, and with Rabbi Benjamin Z. Kreitman, chairman of the Borough President's

Citizens Action Committee for Equal Opportunity, a board which had been set up as a result of the Downstate demonstrations the previous year. Among the others coming in that morning were Dr. Aaron Brown, a member of the Board of Education, Father William Cullen, pastor of St. Peter Claver Roman Catholic Church in the heart of Bedford-Stuyvesant, and Russell N. Service, executive director of the Bedford YMCA, who presumably filled Stark in on the lack of results emanating from Captain Jenkins' meeting at the Y the previous day. It is also presumed that Service and the others told Stark that the rioting, sudden and dramatic as its outbreak might have been, really had been in prospect for many years.

Aroused after his morning conferences—and a look at the headlines in the morning newspapers—Stark called the mayor and Police Commissioner Murphy. They promised him the best possible police protection the city could command, but nothing that would be interpreted as a sign of weakness or as a capitulation to the looters. With that little to work on, Stark called for a meeting at 4 P.M.

Telegrams went out at noon. The recipients were not only those normally considered community leaders, but everybody who might possibly exert some influence on Bedford-Stuyvesant crowds, fifty-seven in all. They ranged from Mrs. Elaine Bibuld, one of the prominent sit-down demonstrators at the Board of Education, protests the previous year and at Downstate (she served a ten-day term for the latter), to Mrs. Ruth Goring, supervisor of the Brooklyn Visiting Nurses Association.

They met at 4 P.M. at Stark's office for three hours in what a public relations man described as a "heated" discussion. Stark told the assembly, "The community itself, since it is closest to the situation, may best know what can be done and how to do it." He immediately found out how

155

wrong he was. The assembled leaders were the first to tell him that at that moment they spoke for no one other than themselves.

Stark's aides, forewarned by the clamor over the Harlem riots, had not expected any easy solutions, but they were shaken by the total lack of reasonable offers. One aide later quoted the position of the Reverend Walter Offutt, minister of Bedford-Stuyvesant's Bethany Baptist Church: "There's nothing that can stop us. If Jesus Christ—if God Himself came down, He would have to shake us pretty hard before we would stop."

Nonetheless, the leaders quickly agreed to forego further street demonstrations and mass meetings "during the period of the emergency" and to exert what personal influence they could—although they insisted repeatedly that the looters and brick-throwers showed little inclination to accept their restraint.

This time it was Assemblyman Tom Jones who used the labor union analogy. Jones shares a law office with Ray H. Williams, Galamison's lawyer, and they usually work together. "The people who are in the streets expressing their discontent won't listen to me," Jones told Stark. "I have not been vested with the power and authority, unfortunately, to make any changes in their lot. I cannot promise them that my appeals will get them jobs."

Yet, in addition to the promised moratorium on demonstrations, Stark did get two further pledges: That those who had sound trucks would use them that night, and that those who were requested would make radio spot announcements urging peace.

Members of the borough president's staff began to contact radio stations shortly after the meeting ended. By 8:40 P.M., the first spot announcement had been made on Radio Station WHN, which put it on the air in a particularly good period during a sports summary immediately preceding the New York Mets game. It was significant that this was the first approach made to the radio and television media. During all the Harlem rioting, nobody had thought to ask radio stations to attempt to open lines of communication with the rioters. The borough president's office aimed for, and received, particular cooperation from radio stations with large teen-age audiences. There were also several spot announcements on television that night, but fundamentally, Stark's assistant, Irving Bykofsky, says, "we wanted to get the disc jockeys. They can reach them in their own language, in a language we don't know how to use."

At Stark's meeting, Brooklyn NAACP announced that it also had a project for "reaching them in their own language." This turned out to be the "Cool It Baby" leaflet. Fleary's law partners, Paul Gibson, Jr., and William C. Thompson drafted it, and NAACP worked all day to get it printed up in time for distribution on Fulton Street before dark. The beginning of the "Cool It Baby" handbill is worth citing in full. It was headed:

Cool It Baby
The Message Has Been Delivered
We have been screaming for jobs, decent schools, clean houses, etc. for years. Some folks just wouldn't listen.

We've been telling them that all hell was liable to break loose unless Negroes saw real progress. Some folks just wouldn't listen.

Today everybody's listening—with both ears.
The Message Has Been Delivered.

Unfortunately, after that beginning, the leaflet trailed off anticlimactically with an appeal for voter registration, hardly the most exciting topic to deprived masses.

What was the most exciting topic to their leaders, how-

157

ever, at least at this time of the day, was Mayor Wagner's delayed decision on a civilian review board for the police. The decision was no.

The mayor's televised talk was an appeal to reason. He noted sensibly that "without law and order, Negro and civil rights progress would be set back half a century. Law and order are the Negro's best friend. Make no mistake about that.

"The opposite of law and order is mob rule, and that is the way of the Ku Klux Klan, the night riders and the lynch mobs."

On and on the mayor talked. He mentioned again his "complete confidence" in Commissioner Murphy and the terrible effect the rioting was having on the tourist business and the World's Fair that the city had invested so heavily in.

The mayor didn't get around to saying what he planned to do about the riots until the end of his televised talk. Then he announced a nine-point program. There was little new in it. The mayor said he had "instructed Commissioner Murphy to insure that police actions against persons beyond the requirements of duty and performance shall be guarded against, and, where occurring, punished."

Another of his points was "full speed ahead with the recruitment and pre-training of minority members for the police services."

And finally, the mayor said he would "exercise my prerogative to review and consider cases of alleged police brutality on the basis of the procedure and review machinery presently established within the Police Department . . ." He proposed to accomplish this review with the aid of Deputy Mayor Cavanagh who would study each case passed upon by the department's own review board headed by Deputy Commissioner Walter Arm.

Nobody thought this would satisfy the civil rights leaders, and the next day, as it turned out, it had not. But on Wednesday night on Fulton Street it would not have made one particle of difference if, as Walter Arm said later, "the mayor had given them Murphy's head—and mine—on a platter."

With the approach of dusk, loungers had already begun to gather on Fulton, and if the mayor's speech had little effect in getting them off the street, neither did it seem to bring anyone onto the street. If you were the kind of person that cared, at all, about what the mayor or any other authority said, then you were not the kind who would participate in riots to begin with.

So the crowds increased, and, as on the previous night, at least nine out of ten came not to riot or loot, but "for a look-see around." What they would do after the glass began breaking was another matter, but Wednesday evening they had something new to gawk at. This was the first visible result of the plans police had been making all day.

The cavalry had arrived.

A troop of mounted policemen had taken over the four corners of Nostrand and Fulton, and occasional pairs of mounted officers were staked out along Fulton. Police had been afraid to use horses in Harlem because of their vulnerability to the Molotov cocktail, but the lower buildings and wider streets in Bedford-Stuyvesant reduced the danger from the rooftops. Yet there were several high points on Fulton Street, three- and four-story apartments over stores. The difference in the situation from that in Harlem did not become apparent to reporters at first; then they realized the further extent of police planning. There were people on the roofs all right, but they were cops.

With police in control of what heights there were, the

159

horses had been vanned over from Manhattan in the hope they would have more effect in controlling the crowds on the corner. And it was true that when the horses headed for someone, he moved. They were effective in keeping auto traffic free, too. On Tuesday night, police had kept cars moving on Fulton; tonight they were determined to keep traffic flowing on Nostrand, Bedford, and Franklin as well.

To help in that aim, they had moved the mobile communications headquarters a block away onto Macon, a side street off Nostrand. The truck was parked behind barriers across the street from the disused Girls' High. And in addition to a new headquarters location there was a new commander. Clerke and Hallinan had gone home after forty-eight hours to get some sleep, and their boss, Anthony S. O'Connell, had been called in from vacation to take charge.

But traffic or no traffic, things were edgy on Fulton Street even before nightfall. Everybody, police, onlookers, and reinforced battalions of reporters and photographers were waiting. And then came an incident that could have —but didn't—set the whole borough aflame. Without notice there were four sharp reports from a height to the north. Sidewalk loungers dove for doorways, police grabbed for revolvers, photographers for cameras.

East and west on Fulton Street the laughter rang. Up on a fourth floor fire escape strutted a little boy with a cap gun.

Shaky, the loungers picked themselves up, the police reseated their revolvers, and the cameramen toyed with the idea of taking the kid's picture for a gag shot, then decided to forget it. The boy's mother seemed to think it was all very funny.

A few sheepish grins, on both sides, released a little of the tension that had been mounting during the day. The little release was not enough, however. It only delayed the battle.

A sound truck pulled onto the street. It was decorated with NAACP voter-registration stickers. Inside it were Fleary and three other NAACP workers. They had been in the area, and on the microphone, since 5:30 P.M., except for a detour downtown to pick up the "Cool It Baby" leaflets. Now Fleary and his three associates were taking turns broadcasting while other NAACP members, including the branch president, Warren Bunn, circulated among the crowds with the leaflet. The NAACP men were easily identifiable; they had donned special overseas caps. "We decided to wear them so people would know the NAACP was out there trying to break up this thing," Fleary says.

The leaflet was very well received by the throngs on the street, and so was the sound truck when at about 7:30 it parked near the spot where the nationalist speaker had stood the night before. Fleary was at the microphone, and he was applauded when he began speaking.

Police interpreted this as a good sign. They breathed a little easier and began to relax. When they looked up a minute later it was dark, and the crowds had increased immeasurably. Thousands jammed the four corners. Several hundred clustered around the sound truck. Still others knotted across the street under the marquee of the Banco Theater.

"I don't want any outside agitators coming in here and destroying this community," Fleary said. "The press has exploded this thing out of proportion. Wallace, Goldwater, every Southern figure is happy at what happened last night."

"Goldwater must go," somebody yelled out. There was a cheer. Fleary, thus encouraged, went on with a plea for a little consideration for the "cop on the beat."

That is when the street started to blow up.

Whether it blew up because the cop on the beat is the symbol of the white power structure to Negroes, or because, as Fleary thinks, a timed signal cued agitation to begin will never be resolved. In either case, that is when agitation did begin. "The guy on the beat is not the guy to take it out on," the NAACP official was saying. "He has a wife and a family and has to support them like you and me. The pressure must be put where it belongs—at the deputy commissioner level. These are the guys to put the pressure on, not the guys on the beat."

Until then, the crowds seemed to have been with him all the way. There were serious nods when Fleary had said that Bedford-Stuyvesant, as opposed to Harlem, was a "community of law," and that "Brooklyn never had anything like this before in its total history." There seemed agreement that the NAACP "understood the problems and had been attacking the problems of the concentrated ghetto . . . we shouldn't confuse New York City with Alabama. . . ." Through all this, the crowd had been, as far as could be determined, almost unanimous in its approval. But, Fleary says, there was one dissenter, a man who kept saying, over and over, "What about police brutality? What about police brutality?"

"Because of the sensitivity of the whole incident [Gilligan-Powell] I did not want to discuss police brutality out on the streets," Fleary says. "I felt it would only inflame the whole climate, but this one guy had friends, and they took up this cry and they kept it up so much that the crowd began to ask the question. Then I knew I had to try to meet the issue head-on." And Fleary met the issue head-on with a defense of the beat cop. It was a defense he never got to finish.

From under the Banco marquee across the street came a group of men. Fleary says that four among them wore green berets, and this testimony on the point is significant. Police have said that the rioting in Harlem and Bedford-Stuyvesant, much of it at any rate, was a planned and organized thing. Newspaper and magazine reporters mentioned agitators with big green sunglasses and walkie-talkies whipping up the mob in strategic spots. Yet in six nights of rioting, Fleary is the only community leader of any stature who can say, "Yes, I saw organized agitators. They were doing thus and so."

What the men Fleary saw were doing, at that moment, was trying to overturn his station wagon. Each of the four had positioned himself at a fender, and they were rocking the car back and forth, rhythmically.

"These guys were in their upper twenties, early thirties," Fleary says. "They wore green berets [similar to the ones worn by Army Special Forces men trained for guerrilla warfare] and when I saw them coming at me, I knew they weren't coming for any good purpose. When they started to rock the station wagon, they knew what they were doing. They got the teen-agers laughing, and then they started to help these men rock us. Then everything got out of hand."

Yes, it did. Police had hesitated to see if this was normal heckling or if Fleary was really in trouble. They could see the station wagon rocking, but the attorney still had possession of the microphone. "Let me finish, please let me finish," he was saying, and then he lost the microphone, too. That was the signal. A flying phalanx of mounted and foot patrolmen charged into the mob to rescue the embattled NAACP men. Knots of the crowd shot out in every direction into the darkness, east and west on Fulton Street, north and south on Nostrand, and after they had passed the distracted cops, the windows started to go again.

Police reached the sound truck; Fleary and the NAACP men were safe, and the cops turned back when the burglar alarms rang. Men and women filled their arms and scuttled into the side streets, Arlington Place, Herkimer Street, and Verona Place. "It was the same stores as before," Mrs. Bryant reported from Herkimer Street. "Those people had put up signs saying the stores were owned by Negroes, but that didn't seem to make any difference."

Garbage cans lined Fulton Street, as they had the night before, and with the first wave of surging men and women this waiting ammunition was swept up; but what to do with it? Most of the windows had been replaced by plywood, and so the rioters looked for new targets. Many cans were aimed at police, on foot, on horses, and in cars. Others were just hurled for the sake of hurling. One shiny new car, being driven by a Negro, was the target of three or four cans as it pulled away from a parking place on the other side of Bedford Avenue. Its rear fender was crumpled by one can accurately thrown by a girl.

The trouble worked its way over to Bedford Avenue. Other women, possibly lacking garbage cans, had, without warning, suddenly descended upon a patrolman, kicking and scratching him and tearing at his shirt. A sergeant moved in to help, and he and the patrolman found themselves surrounded by Negro men chivalrously coming to the aid of the women. One of the men knocked down the sergeant. Both officers pulled their guns and fired into the air. In a minute the street around them was clear.

The crowds ran toward Franklin. There, police had troubles of their own. A man had thrown a can through the window behind them as they surged toward the shots from Bedford, and they had turned back at the crash of glass. By the time they had turned themselves around once more, the crowds streaming from Bedford were upon them.

Officers dropped to one knee to fire in the air, and the tide of runners split. Many tried to stop, but were pushed on by those behind them. Nightsticks rose and fell.

Photographers had by this time driven over from Nostrand Avenue, and one got one of the best pictures of the rioting. It made all the papers the next day. It showed a Negro youth, well dressed, lying momentarily dazed in a gutter as the cops milled around him. One cop was standing over the Negro, nightstick in hand, arm bent as if he had just struck.

Pictures can lie. The Negro in the gutter had slipped and fallen off the curb, tripped up by his own running momentum. The cop with the nightstick had been running full tilt in another direction, and had stopped abruptly to keep from stepping on the prostrate Negro. The other police were attempting to keep an eye on the retreating Negroes running back toward Bedford Avenue. A second after the flash went off, the Negro scrambled to his feet and ran off, if not unscathed, at least unhindered by New York City police.

The following day the *New York Post* ran that picture with a one-line caption, written by a deskman no nearer to the rioting than his office across the river in Manhattan. It read: "Cops wielding nightsticks surround Negro beaten to the ground in Bedford-Stuyvesant."

Negroes were beaten, some brutally, in Bedford-Stuyvesant that night. Yet, for the most part, New York City police operated under the greatest restraint and discipline ever imposed on an American police department, and did it creditably. And it isn't taking anything away from that statement to say that this restraint was most pronounced when the individual officer realized he was under the eyes of his superiors or the press. Cops are human, too.

The provocations were almost intolerable. Not only the verbal ones, but the physical ones. But it would start out verbally in most cases. Men and women would surround a group of police, and then the words would come: "Mother ———," "Go home, whitey." "Come on you ——— you scared, whitey?" The police, officers and men alike, had never taken abuse like this without taking action, and they fingered their nightsticks and ostentatiously put their hands to their holsters, but they were under orders to take it, and they took it. Even minor looting was tolerated. People were taking things from shattered store windows, not so much to take them, but to do it as an insult to the police who were watching them. As Commissioner Murphy said later, every arrest meant another cop off the lines, and that night the police lines in Bedford-Stuyvesant needed every man.

The trouble was, though, that forbearance led to more problems. The insults grew worse and worse as they were ignored. The mob seemed bent on a test of strength. Men and women, speaking from the security of the center of a gang of people, soon turned to physical violence. Bottles, bricks, stones, anything that would serve as a weapon, were hurled. In the darkness police were unable to tell just which man or woman did the throwing, and they would charge, not indiscriminately, but at the biggest men they could find—men who might have been totally innocent of doing anything more than giving support to the mob by their very presence.

One officer who had his reservations about this departmental policy of restraint was Inspector Clerke. "If they want to say terrible things about me," he said later, "let 'em go ahead. But in the long run all this meant that it was just going to gather a crowd bent on force that couldn't be handled."

Police weren't the only targets. Attacked with them were the NAACP leaders, the press, or anyone foolhardy enough to suggest withdrawal. Some of the worst looters were beginning to mutter threats against those who were holding aloof from vandalism.

This was the mob's day, a day when each man on the street was a leader with four thousand followers. NAACP had been determined to show the community it was on the streets trying to stop violence. Even after its sound truck had been driven off, NAACP men continued trying to hand out the leaflets. But now it was as if NAACP had a contagious disease. Hundreds of the mob gathered around the most heavily guarded corner, at Nostrand and Fulton Street, and screamed not only at the police but at the press and at an NAACP man who had retreated there. The NAACP man, Teddy Little, wrestled with himself for minutes. Finally he reached up and regretfully took off his overseas cap, carefully folded it, and placed it in his pocket. "I'm scared to death," he admitted. A Negro who would have been obvious as a detective even without his police helmet came up to Little and flashed his badge. "We're here with you," he said.

Police were chasing up and down and all over Bedford-Stuyvesant. Calls flooded the police switchboard, more than one a minute over a three-hour period. Prowl cars and fire engines rushed from alarm to alarm. And at least eighty percent were unfounded—deliberately turned in, police swear, to lure them away from another looting. This was not always the case, however. Many alarms were calls for help from lawful citizens who saw gangs descend on their corners. If the corners were empty by the time police got there, that didn't mean that the gangs hadn't been there. The grapevine operated efficiently those nights, and people looting stores could be warned in plenty of time to get away, sometimes when police were still three or four blocks off. There would be a series of high-pitched whistles, or sometimes just the call, "The man, look out for the man," and then the sound of running feet, and only an empty corner when the police arrived. The officers would pull up in two or three prowl cars, look around— sometimes they wouldn't even bother to get out of their cars—and radio back, "unfounded." After a while, the prowl cars would leave, and then, gradually, like mice after the cat has passed by, the mob would return.

One of those calls through the police switchboard led police right into an ambush of battles at Broadway and Fulton Street, on the eastern border of Bedford-Stuyvesant. The prowl cars pulled up from various directions, and were met with a barrage of glass, thrown simultaneously from roofs and from the elevated station. One of the bottles broke a police windshield. The others smashed harmlessly onto the streets.

Father Cullen, of St. Peter Claver, was one of the very few white men—if not perhaps the only one—who walked alone in Bedford-Stuyvesant that night. He tells of meeting a small Negro boy, one of his parishioners, running down the street with clothing right from a cleaning store. The boy, about eleven years old, hung his head. "I'm sorry, Father," he said, "but *everybody's* doing it." Then he high-tailed off.

It did seem as if *everybody* was doing it. If it wasn't clothing, it was groceries. Stanley Brezenoff, the white

CORE worker, said, "We saw people going into grocery stores, going into the back, coming out with wide smiles." On Lewis Avenue, the CORE car was stopped across a crosswalk when a Negro man came out of a grocery store with a big loaded carton. "Move it, baby," the man said to the CORE driver. "I got places to go."

It wasn't all that pleasant, though. There were arrests, many of them, and there were casualties. Many of the civilians hurt, Inspector Clerke said later, were men caught red-handed inside stores "who figured they might as well try and fight their way out." Three of these men were shot; the first as he was coming out of a clothing-store window, the second when he was surprised inside a check-cashing establishment, and the third as he fled from a looted liquor store.

As on the previous night, it wasn't always the guy who did anything that was hurt, but rather the one who was too slow in moving. The same was quite often true about those arrested. Like a boy named Prince. His neighbors say he was standing in his own front yard on Lexington Avenue when a gang of boys swept around the corner with stolen shoes. Right behind came the cops. The boys ditched the shoes and took off in all directions. The cops, who had seen the incident differently from the neighbors, quit the chase. After they walked back, they picked up Prince from his own front yard, put him in an arriving prowl car, and then, as an afterthought, threw in a pair of shoes as evidence.

But if the police were indiscriminate sometimes, so, at almost all times, was the mob. Assemblyman Tom Jones, who lives at Dean and Nostrand, had told himself he wasn't going out no matter what happened that night, but he went out. "I didn't have to," he said later. "I am not a policeman; there was nothing I could do. I saw the wreck-

169

age, the undiscriminating attitude of the people. They didn't discriminate between stores owned by Negroes and white people. The kids who came around here don't know the places. Some guys were yelling, 'don't hit that place,' but everybody was not made privy to it. Some knew it, but they couldn't communicate it to everybody.

"I saw them throwing rocks. They would come up, look around, see if a cop was nearby, or sometimes just stand across the street and heave, or they would come running along and heave it running. They'd laugh, and then run away. They didn't even bother to loot. The looters were the moochers and the same elements that operate after floods and catastrophes."

Jones watched for a while, and then went over to Manhattan to appear on a radio discussion show. From the studio, he asked the looters to go home.

Another making broadcasts that night was Father Cullen. He was telephoning spot broadcasts from booths in Bedford-Stuyvesant to the radio stations that Abe Stark's staff lined up: It was Father Cullen, on Wednesday night, who went out to find a leading Negro Protestant minister, the Reverend Richard Martin of St. Philip's Church for a spot-broadcast appeal from a phone booth.

There were, indeed, stories all over the four-square-mile rough parallelogram of Bedford-Stuyvesant, and no way for any man, police statistician, or reporter, to cover them all. A report that everyone tried—fruitlessly—to trace was that of a phantom black and white tow truck cruising the streets of Bedford-Stuyvesant and pulling off the metal gates of stores as a sort of "public service" for looters. One story that reporters did cover took shape at the Gates Avenue stationhouse, headquarters of Captain Jenkins' command. Police would chase a gang up a street, then turn around and pick up the merchandise abandoned by the fleeing looters. Before long, seventy-five phonographs, fifty television sets, chairs, lamps, a cash register, cases of liquor—you name it—made a heap on the ground floor of the stationhouse. Most of the prisoners arrested were being taken to Gates Avenue for booking. So reporters checked in there as often as they could. The problem was in getting there and getting back to Nostrand and Fulton safely, and for the most part the newsmen solved it by driving in pairs or in even larger groups.

Edward Ringer, a reporter for the *New York Times,* was driving from the stationhouse back to Fulton with another reporter, when a group of Negro youths came up to the car as it was stopped for a red light. Nobody else was on the street. "The New York Times" was plainly printed on the side of Ringer's car. It was, in addition, equipped with a revolving dome light.

"You from the press?" the biggest of the Negro boys demanded.

"Yeah," said the reporter with Ringer, checking to make sure the car doors were securely locked. The windows were rolled up, but he was still worried, and, out of the corner of his mouth, he said, "Eddie, let's get out of here."

But the light was red, and the car didn't move. "Eddie," the other reporter said, "the cops won't mind. Go through the light."

"I got a statement for the press," the biggest Negro youth said.

"Eddie," the hitchhiking reporter said, "I'll pay the ticket myself, Eddie. Go through the light."

Still the car didn't move. "You want to take down my statement for the press," the Negro youth said, and it wasn't a question. The reporter reached for his pad. His biggest worry was that the boys would completely surround the car, fore and aft, and make it impossible to

171

move. But the youths didn't. They lounged against the right rear fender, and banged at the windows, but they didn't try to get in front. And eventually the light changed, just as the boy was about to begin his statement. The car pulled away, but the reporter was able to get down every word of it. It wasn't long, but quite clear. "We're gonna kill every one of you white bastards."

After the car turned left onto Nostrand, the frightened reporter threw down his pad on the seat. "Why didn't you go through that light?" he demanded of Ringer, who had not said a word.

"What, in the *Times* car?" Ringer asked.

The other reporter stared at him aghast. "The next time," he said, "I'll ride with the *Daily News*."

It was the rain that ended it.

One minute, thousands clustered outside police lines at Nostrand and Fulton; mounties were making periodic excursions up and down the block to drive back marauders; cameramen were following, lighting up the backs of fleeing figures with their flash bulbs—and the next minute, the flash bulbs were lighting up only empty streets.

The rain began in drops, just after midnight, and by 12:15 the street was empty enough to allow some of the cops a breather. At 1 A.M., the mounties rode out, all of a half block, to the yard of the Girls' High building.

And in the middle of Nostrand and Fulton stood a knot of happy reporters and police. "Rain, rain, rain, rain, come on and rain," one of the cops was saying. A photographer posed him, one hand outstretched, with a happy smile on his face.

"I don't know why it is," one cop said. "Some of these people aren't afraid of horses, of nightsticks, even of guns. A couple of drops of rain and they run."

9

Thursday, July 23

It was over by Thursday night. You could tell it, although there was nothing you could really put your finger on, and police were just as strong as they had been on Wednesday. But it was over.

There were as many people on the corner of Nostrand and Fulton, at least early in the evening, but the mood was changed. It was lighter; the pressure was off. And this despite the fact that it had been a hotter day. The high Thursday had been 87 degrees; on Wednesday it had been 81.

Abe Stark had carried through on his promise to "present the sense" of his Tuesday meeting to Mayor Wagner. But that certainly hadn't made the difference. The radio spot announcements continued, and more Negro ministers joined the "Cool it" drive. Some forty had promised to be on the streets that night, and whether or not all forty kept that promise, Commissioner Murphy was later to commend them for a "terrific job." The police commissioner is not a man who is chary with praise.

And at least two of the ministers did do a "terrific job" in presenting themselves to the people of Bedford-Stuyvesant. They were V. Simpson Turner, executive secretary of the Protestant Council's Brooklyn Division, and R. L. Evans, pastor of the New Friendship Baptist Church at 1825 Prospect Place. These two, in a Department of Sanitation sound truck driven by a patrolman, spent the hours of twilight and darkness driving around and around with the same message of peace. "Will you kindly listen to law and order," they must have said thousands of times, "this is the best for all concerned. Go home now; this is worse than you think."

With the coming of the darkness, the ministers made a point of staying off Fulton Street. Police did not want a repetition of the previous night's incident with the NAACP sound truck. That truck was out again, too, and so were several from political organizations, but it was the white sound truck labeled "Help Keep Our City Clean" that traveled furthest from the core of Nostrand and Fulton and its force of police.

The NAACP sound truck did make a pass along Fulton Street early, determined, as Fleary said, "that there would be no question in anybody's mind that we knew we were doing the right thing." It drew such vociferous heckling that the speaker could not be heard. Yet even though the insults were as vile as the previous night's, the hatred and rancor did not seem as pronounced.

From the middle of the crowd as the NAACP sound truck passed came boys with signs. "We want NAACP to stay out of this, we will see that fifteen-year-old-youth cop killer gets a fair trial," said one. "We will fight now and pray later," said another. A third read, "The dead can't talk, we can." One of the boys with the signs was

174

asked who the "we" was, and he replied, "us, the people."

But he was lying. On this evening, "us, the people" were the gangs. The appearance of the boys with the posters surprised the police.

Most of the rioting had been carried on by young adults, not by teen-age gangs. There had been teen-agers, of course, many of them, but few had seemed to be gang members, and a Youth Board check of those arrested had borne this out. "We've been working hard to make sure they aren't present," Abe Taylor, Brooklyn supervisor for the Youth Board, had said just that day. That night, though, the gang members were out on Fulton Street. A twenty-year-old stood arrogantly on the northeast corner at Nostrand cooperatively pointing out to reporters, "Buccaneers, Bishops, Chaplains, Warlords, Corsairs, tonight they're all around." And there was harmony among them, despite the fact that these were fighting gangs pledged by their perverse ground rules to wage "wars" upon each other. "All the gangs fighting against each other," the youth said. "They aren't fighting now. They're united."

The following day the *Journal-American* ran an exclusive story that "the rampant looting in Brooklyn [is] the work of the warlords of several tough gangs of teen-agers banded together under the name of 'the Defenders'. . . . The looting is completely divorced from any civil rights protests, except that the Defenders are taking advantage of organized agitators, who, by inflaming Negro youths to violence, draw attention away from the looters' operations."

The *Journal-American* story was only partially correct. It was not until this third night that, whether by treaty or just by implicit agreement, the more than one thousand members of the twenty-two fighting gangs recognized by the Youth Board in Bedford-Stuyvesant had decided to declare an armistice among themselves and to try to stir up the mobs. They had help. On Thursday night, the neatly dressed Black Muslims came over from Harlem to hawk copies of their newspaper, *Muhammad Speaks*. The headline on the newspaper was, in the context of the Harlem rioting, as inciting as the makeshift signs of the gang members. It said, "Muhammad Thanks Harlem."

Patrolman Harold Lowe, the man with the Nostrand Avenue post at Fulton identified two youths as gang members. "Don't let me catch you here in a little while," he said to them. The two youths sneered, but "in a little while" they weren't there. Neither were any of the other gang members. About an hour after darkness they had given up trying to arouse the crowds with their signs and their yells, and had returned to their respective "turfs."

The purpose of the gangs was perhaps so obvious as to be self-defeating. If they could have gotten the rioting going again, the gangs would have been free to loot almost at will. But the plan didn't work, perhaps because this sudden conversion of punks to the cause of civil rights and James Powell was so transparent a maneuver as to be plain to everyone.

With the easing of tension on Fulton Street, police extended their patrols, forcing the gang raids farther afield. Another reason the gangs ranged farther afield was simply stated by one police official near the mobile communications headquarters. In the Fulton Street vicinity, he pointed out, "there aren't many windows left to break."

Still, the gangs had planned to loot, and, no matter how risky it appeared, some were determined to loot. Police kept busy chasing them in outlying areas, particularly in

Williamsburg and Bushwick. And when there were no real gangs to chase, there was still that phantom tow truck. Newspaper reports of the truck's free gate-wrenching service had caught the public's fancy. The black and white phantom was blamed wherever metal gates were twisted open. It never was found, however. In many cases, police found that husky looters had merely torn down the thin metal links with their hands.

If police were having to patrol farther out to keep up with the gangs, so were the reporters and photographers who followed the police radio. On this, the third night, all three television networks were represented. Their cameramen and complicated lights augmented a press corps which at this point even included photographer recruits from Italian publications and representatives of foreign wire services. Bedford-Stuyvesant was making its bid for the ill fame of Harlem.

The *Daily News* kept two cars, and occasionally three, working. The *Times* had two cars out. But the one man credited—especially by his own paper—with ranging further afield than any of the others was *Journal-American* photographer Mel Finkelstein. He wasn't the only daring one. The *Herald Tribune*'s pretty girl photographer, Jill Krementz, was so annoyed by her paper's refusal to assign her to the story that she came over on her own, and on Tuesday night at least, came out with the best shots of the rioting. She had been up in Harlem on her own, too—admittedly scared—but she excelled in Bedford-Stuyvesant.

Jill, in her borrowed helmet, black jacket and blue jeans, was a notable target for bottle throwers, but it was Finkelstein who, early Thursday evening, ran into trouble only two blocks from the 79th Precinct station. A store there had been looted earlier, and Finkelstein only gave it a passing glance from the wheel of the *Journal-American* car. But that glance was enough to pick up shadows inside the store. The police were gone, and the looters were back. He eased the car to the curb and reached for his camera. He was spotted at that point by neighboring residents, and down came the barrage. Bottles, bricks, tin cans of food, all were hurled at him. And, literally as a topping, a stolen cake was hurled by one of the looters. One bottle smashed Finkelstein's windshield, and the cake icing also left its mark. Finkelstein dropped his camera after a hurried picture and got out—safely this time. He wasn't always to be as lucky, however. He was hurt three weeks later, along with *Journal-American* reporter Mike Pearl—the friend that Junius Griffin of the *Times* had led to safety up in Harlem—when someone in a mob in Paterson, N.J., hurled a brick through their car window.

Thursday night was also notable in Bedford-Stuyvesant for the arrest of the first and only white civilian involved in the Brooklyn rioting. One of the few remaining white residents of Myrtle Avenue, he was charged with disorderly conduct and resisting arrest. Police said that the thirty-year-old man had cursed and thrown objects at Negroes passing his home.

But there were no signs of the white gangs said to be heading into Bedford-Stuyvesant to make trouble, just as there were no signs of a caravan of Negroes who were reported to be coming up from Philadelphia to "defend" Bedford-Stuyvesant. As a matter of fact, the major casualties of that evening were two Negroes and two patrolmen hurt in a car collision. The Negroes' car was going through an intersection in the northern fringes of the section. It had the green light and struck, at right angles, the police car hurrying to a "disorderly crowd" report which later proved unfounded.

In Bedford-Stuyvesant the rioting and looting was taking its last gasp. It ended at Lewis and Hancock, five blocks south of where Finkelstein's windshield was smashed. At just about midnight, half a dozen boys were looting a store when police pulled up. Only one seventeen-year-old failed to get away. He had been slow in hearing the warning, and when he looked up, police were on him. The boy way slammed up against a police car door and searched—not really with undue roughness; but a crowd formed, egged on by a big Negro woman who kept repeating, "Did you see what those —— did to him? Did you see?"

Police, a little edgy, sounded an "assist officer" call which brought more cars full of police, and they were pushing the crowd back when the ubiquitous Department of Sanitation sound truck with the two ministers pulled onto the scene blaring its message of peace and order.

Nobody paid any attention to the sound truck while the boy was still on the corner. Only when he had been driven away to the precinct station house was its presence recognized. "Ladies and gentlemen, will you please return to your homes," the minister at the microphone was asking, his ignored message echoing up Lewis Avenue. "Help our community, help us make Bedford-Stuyvesant a safe place again. Please return to your homes." He said it over and over again; he wouldn't give up, and finally his voice got under the skin of the big woman who had failed to incite the crowds to act against the police.

Now she turned toward the ministers' truck, possibly thinking of doing physical violence, but police moved to intercept her. Whether this stopped the woman, or she

179

just thought better of attacking the ministers, she stopped, right in the center of the intersection and let loose a stream of invectives. "Go to hell, these are our streets," the woman began, and went on from there. From the look of her, she had barely gotten under way when the rain began. It was starting heavier and even earlier than it had the previous night, and it cut the woman off in mid-obscenity. "Oh-oh," she said, in a normal tone. "Guess I'll go in."

That was the end of the rioting in Bedford-Stuyvesant.

But the rioting in Bedford-Stuyvesant and the earlier rioting in Harlem were not the only matters bedeviling New York City police during that six-day period in July. They also had to contain near-riots at Police Headquarters, of all places.

The CORE pickets at headquarters Tuesday night, had stirred up a hornets' nest among the residents of the predominantly Italian neighborhood which surrounds the headquarters building in downtown Manhattan. The residents, picketing the pickets, proved on Tuesday they knew as many filthy words as the Negroes of Harlem and Bedford-Stuyvesant, and were not any less averse to using them. They also proved they knew how to throw things. An egg splattered on the suit jacket of Deputy Police Commissioner Walter Arm. But on Tuesday that was the major damage.

On Wednesday, the counterpickets came armed with more than eggs. Bottles, firecrackers, and brick fragments were thrown at men and women. Police had to be called from all over downtown to protect the pickets who were there to protest "police brutality." One twenty-one-year-old CORE girl was hit with a broken bottle, and a patrolman almost lost an eye to another piece of broken glass

180

before police could get the hundred or so CORE pickets safely into the IRT subway station at Spring Street.

On Thursday night, police erected barricades to keep the pickets and the counterpickets away from each other. Youths behind the barricades were shouting such things as "Gilligan was right" and "Goldwater for President" and hurling eggs and rocks over the cops' heads toward the pickets. Seven youths were arrested after they threw a sign out of a car at the pickets' feet. The cardboard sign read, "Goldwater Hurry—Get the Smelly Black Basterds [sic] Off This Block."

Police Commissioner Murphy was on hand at headquarters that night—after having taken a look at Bedford-Stuyvesant—and he came out to the barricades to find, as he tells it, "one big guy jumping up and yelling, 'Murphy is our hero. Murphy is our hero.' There was a cop standing next to me, and his jaw was down to his chest. 'I know that guy,' the cop told me. 'I've sent him away ten times myself.'"

There were three clergymen at Police Headquarters Thursday night, two Protestant ministers, Michael Allen, of St. Mark's In-the-Bouwerie and David Romig of the Sea and Land Presbyterian Church on Henry Street, and a Catholic priest, Father Robert Perrella, of the Church of the Most Precious Blood. All three went through the mob—estimated at 1,500 at that point—getting parishioners to go home. Father Perrella won particular praise. One police official told him he was "worth five hundred cops."

Partly because of the clergymen, and partly because police outmaneuvered the counterpickets—hustling the CORE demonstrators south to the subway at Canal Street instead of north to the nearer entrance at Spring Street— there was only one casualty Thursday, typically, a policeman. Inspector Henry Yack required hospitalization after being hit in the right eye with a brick.

The white mob, cheated of its victims, hauled six Negroes—who had nothing to do with any demonstration —off a BMT subway at Canal Street, but police intervened before any serious damage was done. Commissioner Murphy, on hand for at least part of this, was asked why police did not treat the downtown mob as "harshly" as they had Harlem and Bedford-Stuyvesant rioters. "I don't consider this violence at all," he said. "There's a lot of shouting and talking here, but nothing to compare with what's been going on in Harlem and Bedford-Stuyvesant."

What had been going on in Harlem was the end of a riot. The rain had not arrived over there in time to end it as abruptly as in Bedford-Stuyvesant, so the rioting sputtered on for several days. Some of the sputters were the work of militants who were more effective there. In Harlem, unlike Bedford-Stuyvesant, militants did not rely on boys to do men's work.

They did, however, work on the boys—and the girls—as much as possible, and on Tuesday evening the beginning of the end involved a group of teen-agers who had gathered in front of a record shop near CORE headquarters. They were waiting for something as they twisted to the records played over the loudspeaker and swapped stories about the rioting. They were also glancing uneasily among themselves from time to time, each wondering if his partner or his neighbor might not be an FBI "infiltrator." President Johnson had entered the riot picture that day by announcing he was sending the FBI to investigate the Harlem rioting. He called Acting Mayor Screvane and told him the Federal government wanted to help "in this time of agony" in Manhattan.

"American citizens have a right to protection of life and limb—whether driving along a highway in Georgia, a road in Mississippi, or a street in New York City," the President said. Screvane welcomed the action. He said there seemed to be Communist money behind the riots, but later retracted some of his statements.

The kids twisting on 125th Street didn't know whose money was behind anything, and if they had known it is doubtful that they would have cared. They had been well organized, however, and apparently well briefed, too, because at about 9:30 P.M., without any sign of obvious direction, they formed up, started flashing the "Gilligan Wanted for Murder" posters and marched away. They went west to St. Nicholas Avenue, crossed to the south side of the street, turned back to Eighth Avenue and marched south.

Sullivan followed them past the police lines at the barricade at 123rd Street and, a block later, realized that he had literally gone beyond the pale. At the corner of 122nd Street, there were no cops in sight—nothing but a sullen crowd which included a rather attractive Negro woman with a rather unattractive sentiment. "Whiteys are no ——— good," she yelled at him. Sullivan crossed the street as though he hadn't heard her, looked at the disappearing crowd of teen-agers, and then turned casually back up Eighth Avenue to walk the short block to safety. He made it with no further attention from the crowd, but a woman who passed him told her male companion he "oughtta kill that whitey."

One-hundred and twenty-fifth Street hadn't seen the last of the crowd of teen-agers, however. They had crossed over to St. Nicholas Avenue, picked up a little steam, and were coming up St. Nicholas, waving the posters and chanting. At 124th Street, bottles were thrown and police began moving in, firing into the air. The youngsters scattered with delighted whoops.

At 125th Street and St. Nicholas Avenue, Bayard Rustin was in deep conference with Percy Sutton, Democratic nominee for the Assembly. Rustin was asked about youths with walkie-talkies who had once again begun to appear on the Harlem streets, and he said they were part of a group he had organized Sunday night to try to break up crowds. The radio operators were supposed to roam Harlem, reporting crowds of youngsters. Older people would then be sent to talk the youths into dispersing. Rustin introduced Kert Samplez, who was in charge of the patrols.

Samplez, a handsome and straightforward man, attempted to explain the attitude of Harlemites. "They're frustrated," he said. "I've been living in Europe, but I felt I had to come back to my people because they need me. And now look at me, I'm just as frustrated as any of these hippy-dippy kids wandering around here."

"I'm pretty frustrated myself," said a white man.

Later, Samplez, well dressed, respectable in appearance, and obviously not a thrill seeker, tried to get a message from Bayard Rustin to the attention of a police inspector. But lower-ranking officers, who could not see past the color of his skin, made a point of snubbing him. He swallowed it gamely, and kept trying throughout the night to establish some sort of liaison between civil rights people and police.

At that point police needed little liaison. They were preoccupied with a barrage of bottles from the rooftops at 115th Street and Lenox Avenue. Sirens screamed and prowl cars appeared. Police leaped out and charged into the crowds behind a short, round detective, who, except for

184

his helmet and club, might have been a Shriner who had strayed uptown from the national convention then in session. What had caused the show of force here? Why was this crowd being broken up when others were allowed to form unchecked? A young cop at the corner explained that it was the bottles, thrown by the crowd at the police, and by punks from the roofs at everybody. "They throw bottles from the rooftops and windows," he said. "They couldn't hit us because we were back against the buildings, so they threw at their own people. They're crazy."

On one of the corners, a television shop had its gate half drawn across the door, but employees were still inside, sitting around long past quitting time. "Who wants to get caught in a mess like that?" asked one.

A taxicab sped up to the corner and disgorged a woman in a nurse's uniform and a man in white. The nurse was wearing a CORE armband. They said something about an injured woman. A newspaperman asked what it was about and the nurse screamed, "I don't know!" Where had she heard about a wounded woman? "Ask the fuzz!" she screamed.

On Eighth Avenue, a well-lighted bar with a few quiet patrons looked like a possible beer stop for a hot, thirsty whitey. It proved hospitable.

The bartender was teasing a customer, a short, light, handsome man who grinned as the bartender pointed out that he had left after announcing he was going home, and had been back in less than two minutes. "You hadn't any more than gone around that corner before I saw you comin' back takin' those lo-ong steps," the bartender said. "You really like this place, don't you?"

The customer took it in good spirit. "You turn a corner and here comes a gang of kids yellin' and whoopin' and a

185

gang of cops after them with billy clubs," he said. "You can't keep goin'; you gotta either go back or get run over."

The bartender began to express disgust for the riots. He called them "that shit." "It ain't doin' anybody any good," he said. "We had some people in here last night that started talkin' that shit and I went to the boss and told him and he closed up."

Militant civil rights leaders might dismiss these men as Uncle Toms, but to the visiting whitey, they sounded very much like white working men annoyed by small time crooks or the actions of the younger generation. In fact, they blamed the rioting on teen-agers and the underworld, much as police did.

"These riots make a paradise for dope addicts and thieves," the bartender said. "Our kids break the windows and the junkies grab everything inside. They gotta steal to feed their habit, and this makes it easy for them.

"If the parents would take charge of the kids, they couldn't get mixed up in this. These kids are out of school now and they got nothing to do but spend the whole day gathering bottles, making Molotov cocktails and bombs and all those little playthings, just waiting for the night."

The customer couldn't blame the youngsters. "They got all these influences working on them," he said. "They got the civil rights groups, they got the nationalist groups, they got the churches and they got the newspapers. The civil rights groups feed them . . . well, they feed them— shit! The nationalists feed them shit; the churches feed them shit. And those newspapers. . . .

"I'm pretty well off. I got a job, I live all right, I'm happy. But I pick up the paper and start reading it, and all of a sudden I find myself saying, 'Those dirty rotten bastards! They can't do that to us!' No wonder these kids get mixed up in that shit."

"Somebody's got posters out sayin' Lieutenant Gilligan is wanted for murder," said the bartender. "They must have printed up thousands of them."

"Them commies work fast," said the customer.

The trouble died down on Lenox Avenue and a breeze came out of New Jersey about 11 P.M., making the steel police helmets bearable for the first time since the rioting started. Presumably, it also made tenement beds bearable, because the streets began to clear. Rustin said his crowd-control units had helped and added that he thought the rioting was over.

The civil rights leader was asked if he thought the riots had been organized. "I can smell organization in Harlem," he said, "and this has not been organized."

A pair of detectives standing in uniform in front of the Theresa Hotel agreed that the trouble was almost all over. However, they thought there might be a renewal when the grand jury cleared Lieutenant Gilligan. Why were they so sure he would be cleared?

"Listen, if there'd been anything wrong in that case, he'd have been suspended and arrested on the spot," one of them said. "You can't get away with funny business in this department nowadays. Policemen have to obey the laws, too."

Even though the breeze seemed to have ended the real action by early Wednesday morning, sporadic calls did continue to come in. Answering one of them, police found a teen-ager at 114th Street and Eighth Avenue passing out mimeographed sheets entitled "Harlem Freedom Fighters" and containing directions on "How to make a Molotov cocktail."

                    INSTRUCTIONS:
                 ANY EMPTY BOTTLE
                 FILL WITH GASOLINE
                 USE RAG AS WICK
                 LIGHT RAG

                                        TOSS
                                        AND
                                  SEE THEM RUN!

Police got to the boy who was giving out the leaflets
before he had distributed many—and most of the Harlemites who had taken them had dropped them like fire
when they saw what they were. Nonetheless, whoever
had given the boy the leaflets to deliver achieved results
beyond his highest expectations when, on Wednesday, the
Journal-American reproduced his leaflet for all of Harlem
and Bedford-Stuyvesant to see. Actually, although the
other papers tried to avoid giving the "directions" for the
Molotov cocktail, there was no reason for the *Journal-
American* not to spread them across three columns. In
this day and age there were very few people in Harlem
or Bedford-Stuyvesant, or anywhere else for that matter,
who don't know what a Molotov cocktail is and who could
not make one if they had the inclination.

But leaflet or no leaflet, Harlem was nearly a ghost
town on Wednesday night. A few people listened to tran-
sistor radios or watched television sets in public places
as Mayor Wagner made his appeal for law and order. Then
they seemed to go home.

The center of what activity there was was the Harlem
Labor Center, where a meeting of "civil rights groups"
was being held. Reporters who showed up for the meeting found the conservative element reasonably well rep-

                        188

resented, but they also saw the faces of Edward Mills Davis and other black nationalists. The press was duly ejected and told to come back in forty minutes when an announcement would be made. This meeting was to bring the birth of a catch-all organization now known as the Harlem Unity Committee, and the labor was difficult. Reporters who came back in forty minutes had to wait more than three hours, hearing muffled shouts behind the door, before they were invited in for the official announcement, made by Davis, James Lawson, another black nationalist, and two Muslims who were joining with the regular and irregular civil rights organizations as a unified committee.

They were telegraphing Mayor Wagner, attorney Percy Sutton said, demanding his "immediate presence in the Harlem area to discuss and act upon the many ills that affect the community and receive from the group a program that will be the solution to the problems.

"We are also calling upon the mayor for the removal of Commissioner Murphy, Deputy Commissioner Arm and the unnamed inspector in charge of the riot squad that presided over Harlem during the rioting.

"We further demand that Lieutenant Gilligan be dismissed and that the riot squad and all other cops not normally assigned be removed from Harlem."

The demand for the ouster of the genial deputy commissioner, Walter Arm, was a surprise. Why pick on a man who holds what is, in effect, only a public relations job? Sutton explained that the group was angry at Arm because of what he called "public distortions" issued by him during the rioting. "At least 50 percent of the statements he made as fact are incorrect," another member of the group announced.

What if their demands were not met? "We will act," said Sutton. What actions? "We did not reach agreement to announce what actions we will take," said Sutton.

At the 28th Precinct, there was amusement over the addition of Arm's name to the list of those who had to go. "Maybe you'll get a promotion," reporters told the captain from Arm's office who was presiding over the press room. He failed to see the humor of the suggestion. "Who aren't they mad at?" he asked.

On Thursday night, at the bar on Eighth Avenue, they were still talking abot "that shit" but there were more customers. One was a technical worker in a city hospital who wondered, like quite a few other people, in Harlem and out, why no one kept the children at home. His wonder led to reminiscenses of a Depression childhood in Hell's Kitchen on the West Side.

"When I was a kid, we played in the street in our own block, and grownups hung out of the windows of the lower floors and watched us, and you'd better behave or you were going to hear about it," he said. "In Hell's Kitchen we all lived together and got along together— Negroes, Irish, Italians, Jews, everybody. We'd have troubles with kids on other blocks, but if I got ganged by some of them, all the kids from my block came to help. There wasn't any color or race involved. We'd all play together around Sacred Heart Church. Then I went to the Army and went South. The first time I was ever called a nigger was in the Army."

The man from Hell's Kitchen was asked if he really had been happy in such a tough neighborhood. "We were a lot poorer, but we got along together and we didn't hate each other," he said.

The reporter reluctantly left the bar for the streets of

Harlem, where police had doffed their helmets and were in much smaller numbers. There were so few in fact that the white men there, mostly newsmen, felt less comfortable than they had when the bottles were flying Monday night,

Back at the 28th Precinct, things were settling down to a routine, and a young Negro woman carrying a flag staff which looked like a spear passed unchallenged into the station. Upstairs, the captain who had issued communiqués for the press had been recalled. A few reporters presided there over what was, to all intents and purposes, a dead riot. Music began to permeate the room and it finally dawned on them that it was not coming from a radio.

The desk lieutenant nodded. "It's the Police Athletic League Drum and Bugle Corps practicing," he said. "They're pretty good."

They were, too. The next day they won an interstate contest.

10

The Truce

So it was over, for the time being, and probably for the summer in Harlem and Bedford-Stuyvesant, but it was just beginning for the United States. The charge that had been shaped to explode in the New York City ghettos was tested and confirmed in the fury of half a dozen cities.

These riots seemed to establish a recipe for riots. Take one ghetto, add lack of opportunity for either physical or emotional escape, mix in an unsympathetic attitude on the part of society, and heat.

Some time after dark, these elements will jell into a mass thick enough almost to be tangible. Then add a spark. It does not matter what the spark is. It can be something like the killing of James Powell, important because it involves the taking of a human life. Or it can be something as routine as a police attempt to move a stalled car, which is what set Philadelphia off.

And it takes one man—or woman, or teen-age girl—to set the riot unalterably in motion. That person is, as James Baldwin points out in *The Fire Next Time,* someone who feels a need to regain, at any cost, the sense of his own worth. "People cannot live without this sense; they will do anything whatever to regain it. This is why the most dangerous creation of any society is that man who has nothing to lose. You do not need ten such men—one will do."

What stops a riot?

Three days and nothing else. It is like a disease, apparently, that takes three days to check. There are no miracle drugs, no magic formulas that will bring it under control until those three days are over. Until then, the most a civil or police authority can hope for is containment.

This isn't to say that police, civic, social, and religious leaders of the community will not—or should not—try to stop the rioting. It is just that experience seems to show that rioting of this nature takes three days to work itself out, no matter what. The exception is the Harlem riot of 1943 which took six lives but which worked itself out within twelve hours in a spasm of violence and looting.

The granddaddy of all American riots, the draft riots of 1863, followed this three-day-rule of rioting. Dissatisfaction with the draft—and the clause which allowed a rich man to buy his way out for $300—wreaked a havoc in New York that this country had never known before, and prayerfully, may never know again. It began when the first numbers were drawn for the draft call. There was a spark in the drawing itself, and the fighting which broke out scattered an infantry company. The police commissioner was beaten nearly to death. Some of his men *were* beaten to death. Buildings, including an orphanage, were burned. Negroes unfortunate enough to be found were beaten and some of them were hanged.

It started on a Monday and ended on Thursday when three regiments called off the front lines arrived in New York. The mobs achieved nothing, although a great many rioters reduced their poverty somewhat.

The number killed in this mess is not known. Guesses range from 18 (the number of Negroes hanged) to 12,000. Most accepted guess is about 1,200. And these, of course, were white rioters.

There is an interesting contrast between the shocked reactions of 1964 reporters to the use of nightsticks and the reaction of an anonymous *New York Tribune* reporter in 1863. The newsman of a century ago spoke joyfully of the use of the "locust" and became lyrical when he told of police cornering a gang on a roof, beating them unconscious and throwing them like sacks of potatoes down several flights of stairs until they ended up in the street. Yet one young reporter's reaction to his first sight of nightsticks in use at 125th Street and Lenox Avenue was, "I'd never believed in police brutality before."

American attitudes on the use of the nightstick by police have changed since the 20's and 30's when a cop banging a man over the head with a club in a movie comedy was a sure-fire laugh. Maybe Americans have started empathizing with the man who is hit rather than the one doing the hitting.

And perhaps it is the same change of attitude that has given impetus to the civil rights movement.

And if it is ironic that the Negro has waited until he was on his way toward complete integration into society before attacking society, it is equally ironic that the symbol of his attack, the policeman, is of a higher caliber than ever before in American history. The New York Police Department, like other major police departments, is extremely wary of the men it hires and it takes pains to screen out the sadists who, in former times, got their kicks in police work. And in New York City the screening seems to have been successful. Some of the people who are accustomed to being arrested in various places say that New York cops aren't bad at all.

Yet New York cops are tough because New York is tough. Harlem is by no means the only place in New York where a cop can get killed. The New York patrolman walking his beat keeps his eyes open and his ears listening, wherever he is in the city. When someone offers to fight him, a New York cop fights back hard, because he needs to win, but the odds are that he doesn't prolong the fight after he has won it.

Before the riots, a major cry of civil rights leaders was that there weren't enough cops in Harlem and Bedford-Stuyvesant to give sufficient protection to Negro property-owners. Their complaint was to some extent justified.

Negro crime—offenses by Negroes on the persons and property of Negroes—gets short shrift in the New York City courts, press, and Police Department. Newspaper deskmen still ask, "White or black?" before deciding how much space to allot a crime story.

Concurrently, some of the worst discrimination practiced in this country today is practiced against dead or wounded Negroes when their assailants go to court. The light sentences meted out for Negro murders, police feel, do nothing to discourage killing of Negroes by Negroes. It is almost as if the white community is saving its massive deterrents—the death sentence and life imprisonment —for use against those who would take the more highly valued life of a white man or woman.

Some of this is the fault of the Negro community, which

has not yet reached the stage where it is ready to throw its full weight into the fight against Negro crime. Negroes have not yet produced a Carrie Nation who would take a hatchet to the shooting galleries for addicts, the policy banks, and the gin mills.

If James Powell had been stabbed to death in a random, wanton murder on one of Harlem's high-crime street corners, there would, without doubt, have been no outcry. Anyone who might have read about it in the Negro newspapers, the *Amsterdam News* or the *New York Courier*, would have said, "Isn't that too bad," and would have turned the page.

One reason no such cleanup has taken place is that integration in the city of New York has progressed to the point where it is easier for a Negro leader to switch neighborhoods than fight. Most Bedford-Stuyvesant leaders live in integrated Crown Heights. Most Harlem leaders pack up at the end of the day and head for Queens or Westchester.

It is worth noting that the house provided by the Black Muslims for Malcolm X—before the schism in the black nationalist movement—is in Queens. But the pluperfect example of absentee leadership is, of course, Representative Adam Clayton Powell who rules Harlem while commuting between his home in Puerto Rico and his office in Washington. Much of the reason for Representative Powell's political success is the fury that this absentee leadership arouses in the white community. Negroes can take a vicarious delight in what "Ol' Adam" gets away with. And "Ol' Adam" does seem to keep getting away with it. He recently pulled a few political wires and took control of the $117 million HARYOU bonanza right out of the hands of Dr. Kenneth Clark, a nationally known psychologist on the staff of City University. Dr. Clark lives in Westchester County.

A bank clerk in Sullivan's "hospitable bar" put it this way:

"Nobody speaks for me. Jackie Robinson can't speak for Harlem because he lives off in Connecticut and anyway he's better than I am. The guy who lives next door can't speak for me, because he is no better than I am. Roy Wilkins can't speak for me; he doesn't live in Harlem."

This being the case, why do so many people try to speak for the Negro community? This question was put to a Negro reporter waiting, with others, for the multitude of self-proclaimed Harlem leaders to organize themselves into the Harlem United Committee. His answer was that the would-be speakers "want the power that comes when the white people accept them as Negro leaders."

The real leaders of Harlem and Bedford-Stuyvesant are not usually those who cry "police brutality." They are, understandably, the ones who feel police protection—the more of it the better—is a good thing. "All of us want protection," Assemblyman Bertram Baker, long-time representative of Bedford-Stuyvesant in the State Legislature believes. "If we believe anything is going to happen, our first impulse is to call the cops. Sometimes in the very act of protecting the community the policeman endangers his own life. . . . The very community that calls on him for protection is the first to cry police brutality."

Nonetheless, there is such a thing as police brutality. It is going on today—hopefully in decreasing amounts—and it is practiced as it has always been practiced against those in the community who exert insufficient social pressure to fight it. In America, this primarily means Negroes.

Police brutality, as such, takes three forms: Unnecessary beating of a prisoner during an arrest, torture of suspects to elicit confessions, and stationhouse beatings of troublesome prisoners.

Americans have always been inclined to wink at the tortures practiced to obtain confessions, and have lumped them under the euphemism "third degree." The diminution of what is, by any name, torture, has been caused more by lawyers and courts in recent years than by any public outcry.

The incidence of stationhouse beatings varies from city to city as more and more courts take the cold view that assault by a police officer is a criminal offense. As a consequence some cops have become more subtle in finding ways to hurt a man without leaving a mark.

In some jurisdictions, where the old ways are still in force, they aren't so careful about not leaving marks. An additional charge of resisting arrest is usually placed against a defendant if his condition after the beating is serious enough to cause comment.

Stationhouse beatings occasionally take place on sheer moral grounds: Inflicted by police who feel themselves morally superior to defendants charged—charged, not necessarily guilty—with such degrading crimes as child molestation. Professional criminals are rarely beaten on moral grounds. Another factor which encourages these beatings is the occasional assignment as turnkeys and jailers of policemen who are being punished for misdeeds of one kind or another.

There are also ways to mistreat a prisoner on the street. One was demonstrated in front of CORE headquarters on the third night of the Harlem rioting. A man who had thrown a bottle was rushed across the street by four policemen holding him erect, and then heaved—hard—at the squad car. Nobody but a midget will go into an American automobile erect, and the top of the car caught the prisoner on the chin, as the police must have known it would.

There is another area in which police are not above error, and that is in their statistics. Police statistics depend on whom you talk to, and when you talk to them. In Bedford-Stuyvesant, for instance, the day-to-day figures as reported by the precinct or mobile headquarters were:

	TUESDAY A.M.	TUESDAY P.M.	WEDNESDAY	THURSDAY	TOTALS
Injuries	1	23	3	4	31
Arrests	30	105	122	24	281
Broken windows	30	500+	400	40	970+

Yet, when it was all over, police added their figures up and headquarters released these totals for Bedford-Stuyvesant:

Injuries	18
Arrests	302
Broken windows	405

The only total that comes anywhere near to adding up is the number of arrests, and arrests are a relatively hard and fast matter. Either a man is arrested or he isn't. Not so with injuries. A man may be taken away as hurt, and yet refuse hospitalization, and another may think a wound or an injury insignificant and not realize for some time that he has been seriously hurt.

As to broken windows, how do you figure them? Do you count a store with five windows, all broken, as one or five?

Deputy Commissioner Walter Arm ascribes the differ-

199

ences in totals to duplications in the early reports which were ironed out later. It is true that in the riot situation, units operate pretty much without regard to precinct boundary lines. Nonetheless, it would appear that there was a deliberate attempt by police, on all levels, to downgrade much of the rioting statistics. The authors disagree, however, with the Harlem Unity Council which demanded Arm's ouster on the grounds that at least half the things he said were untrue. That charge is patently false; Arm does not say things that are untrue. There are, though, occasions when he doesn't say anything at all, and these occasions give rise to one-sided reports.

As far as the statistics go, however, in all due fairness to the deputy commissioner, he, too, operates on the basis of reports from the precincts and the patrol headquarters, and the tendency to downgrade crime statistics is something inbred in police officials. High reports of crime—and low reports of arrest—will cause captains and inspectors to find themselves put out to pasture. Put the differences in totals down to human nature.

At the other end of the spectrum is the press. If the Police Department tended—because of its system—to downgrade rioting statistics, then the press—because of its system—tended to upgrade them.

During the New York rioting, crime and violence were taking place, and therefore there was news in Harlem and Bedford-Stuyvesant, and no news-gathering source is going to be satisfied with anything less than the most complete—and most colorful—story.

While there is no question that white reporters and photographers, the only unarmed whiteys on the streets, made attractive targets, there is also no question that, at times, there was a tendency for them to overplay their own parts. Rioting makes an attractive selling point for newspapers caught in the middle of the summer doldrums. Riots lead to pictures and headlines which sell papers and in turn lead to more rioting. Not all the rioting, nor all the reporting, is really genuine.

There was a tendency, for instance, among radio and television reporters to make their microphones and cameras available to any militant rights leaders who would come to them, and to use every word they said, unedited, unchecked for truth or possible incendiarism. They had been doing this for months. "You turn on the 6:30 news, and what do you see but Jesse Gray, day after day," said a police official after the Harlem rioting.

But if interviewing Jesse Gray, day after day, was surface reporting, there was also spurious reporting, of the type represented by an Associated Press dispatch bylined by a local reporter. Approximately 360 words moved on the AP's major wire about what it was like to live in "a neighborhood of fear." The reporter who signed that story lives in a housing development on the site of what used to be Ebbets Field. It is about a mile from the nearest rioting. Coincidentally, the Ebbets Field project is also Shapiro's home, and when he reached it after the nights of the riots, it seemed peaceful. The AP story received widespread play in the South, where news media were emphasizing everything they could about the Northern race riots. Many of these were papers which had recently blasted their Northern colleagues editorially for sensationalizing Southern civil rights violence.

Of course, not every newsman was eager for any part of the rioting story. This reluctance increased after *New York Times* photographer John Orris was hurt in Harlem, and Mel Finkelstein and Mike Pearl were hurt in Paterson. It became only too plain that the casualty rate among the noncombatant newsmen was higher, in proportion, than that of police or rioters.

One photographer, who had covered Bedford-Stuyvesant and Jersey City, was nearly fired for refusing to accept another riot assignment. Ironically, that one never came off. It had been threatened for Hicksville, Long Island.

Why wasn't there a riot in Hicksville or South Jamaica, L.I., or in Newark, N.J., or in the East Bronx, or in any one of the more than fifty American ghettos where the recipe for rioting has been followed to the letter? Was it that the ministers were especially active in South Jamaica or the Negro political leaders in Newark? Probably not.

It was two things. The first was the lack of the spark, or police incident to serve as a spark. In this context, both the Harlem and Bedford-Stuyvesant riots can be said to have followed the rallies initiated by CORE. Granted that in Harlem CORE speakers were succeeded on the platform by speakers of more militant organizations. Still it was CORE that provided the platform, and the respectable backing which drew many to the rally in the first place.

"If you make an inflammatory speech and then tell everybody to go home, you have struck the match," said Dr. Sandy Ray. "With the climate the way it is, the one who makes inflammatory statements bears a lot of responsibility."

The second reason that riots did not break out in many areas was the proximity of these areas to the sites of previous riots. Those with the inclination to mix themselves up in riots tended to go where the riot was, rather than wait for the chance to start rioting on their own home grounds.

But the rioting progressed across America, erupting in city after city where the fuses were lit.

These riots, following the pattern of those in Harlem and Bedford-Stuyvesant, went on despite a divergence in tactics by both police and Negro leaders. And although they offered scant benefit to their communities, they did provide a yardstick to measure New York City police during the rioting.

The principal issue is the question of gunfire. New York City police did not stint on ammunition. They fired in the air, sometimes on scant provocation, to break up crowds. "This was deliberate firing in the air," Commissioner Murphy says. "These men were kneeling, being careful. Nobody was running down the street going boom, boom, boom. What these shots prevented was hand-to-hand combat; in hand-to-hand you will have a lot of deaths and injuries." (The commissioner was somewhat mistaken: his men did fire on the run.)

The combined statistics of the Harlem and Bedford-Stuyvesant riots and the downtown violence as well, appear to back him up. In New York City, over the six-day period, police statistics show 1 man killed (the Harlem brick thrower), 118 police and civilians injured, and 465 men and women arrested.

When rioting first broke out in New York, civil rights leaders said there was no rioting in Rochester and Philadelphia because those towns had civilian review boards. Rioting in both those towns destroyed that argument and even turned it against itself. Possibly because of the civilian review boards, police in Rochester and Philadelphia did not draw their guns, and injury totals were much higher. In Rochester, police turned and ran away from mobs, leaving newsmen behind, unprotected. In Philadelphia, police took no action at all against looters operating before their very eyes. In Philadelphia, a cop spotted a brick thrower with an arsenal who was peppering crowds from above. "Can I get an order to shoot this bum off the roof!" he radioed. The answer came back: "Hold your fire."

Probably the greatest example of differing positions in riot tactics was the simultaneous trouble in Paterson and Elizabeth, N.J. In Paterson, Mayor Frank X. Graves, Jr., took personal command, barking orders over police megaphones, making one of the forty-three arrests himself.

In Elizabeth, where Mayor Steven J. Bercik took no part in the police action, but allowed his men to fire warning shots when necessary, injuries and arrests were fewer. The duration was identical.

In the light of the Philadelphia rioting, Roy Wilkins asked the Federal Department of Justice to investigate the possibility that the riots might have been planned, on some kind of an assembly line, mass production basis.

Noting quite correctly that riots and "brazen looting" had "brought shame upon the civil rights movement of a whole people," Wilkins said, "the suspicion is widespread that they have been planned, and that people have been paid to start and keep them going."

CORE Director James Farmer and the Urban League's Whitney Young, Jr., seconded the call for such a probe, although both said they had no evidence to support the suggestion. Young indicated that he felt that the rioting would benefit Communist and right-wing groups by "sowing confusion and creating hostility between whites and Negroes."

The civil rights leaders were not the only ones who thought of this possibility. A New York City official revealed that undercover men from the Bureau of Special Services had a tip, never publicly confirmed, that right-wing money, funneled through black nationalists, was used to organize this rioting.

One element, interpreted by many as a sign of organization, was the mystifying absence of guns and knives among the rioters.

One gun was seized on Thursday, July 23, as the riots were dying out in Bedford-Stuyvesant. It was a loaded Mauser in the Theresa Hotel room which is the headquarters of Malcolm X's Muslim Mosque, Inc., but the room was empty when it was raided, and no arrests were made.

Yet in Bedford-Stuyvesant alone, police had mentioned 40,000 guns, and a newspaper reported that automatics were being bought and sold on Fulton Street for $25.

James X, a Brooklyn militant, finds much to be happy about in this. "What they expected in Harlem was that Malcolm and the black nationalists would break out their guns, but they did not. This destroyed the cops.

"That's why they broke into Malcolm's place because they did not know what was in the air. All this builds up more fire. How many guns did they capture? One. This is what is worrying the Police Department."

What was worrying the New York Police Department, and presumably the FBI after President Johnson's order bringing it in, was where the money came from to print up the "Gilligan Wanted for Murder" posters, and the "How to Make a Molotov Cocktail" throwaways.

One argument against any widespread organization was the startling maturity of most of those arrested in the Harlem and Bedford-Stuyvesant rioting. Militants make good use of kids—witness the march from CORE headquarters in Harlem Tuesday night. Yet there were 465 riot-connected arrests in Harlem and Bedford-Stuyvesant. Only 25 of those picked up were under sixteen; another 56 were sixteen or seventeen, and 81 were between eighteen and twenty. But 175 of those arrested were between twenty-one and twenty-nine, and 128 were over twenty-nine.

But if there was organization, there was also anticipation—preparation by Negroes for the trouble they knew would come sooner or later.

This kind of preparation did not require a leaflet, or even a word of command. These riots were coming, they were in the air; tension thick enough to slice hung over the steaming streets. Many a ghetto resident, especially after the first day of trouble in Harlem, wondered what he would do when the fighting came his way. And too many answered the question by caching away a supply of bricks or Molotov cocktails on the roof or by the front window of an upper-story apartment, not to start anything, mind you—but just in case the ——— fuzz comes this way.

Aside from the court actions which presumably enriched the lawyers, and the short-term gain of looting, what had the rioters of Harlem and Bedford-Stuyvesant accomplished?

For one thing, they had cost the people of New York City a great deal of money. Extra police expenses—mostly overtime pay—came to $1,500,000. Within a month after the riots ended, damage suits totaling $2,500,000 had been filed against the city.

The riots had made a reality of the white backlash. Anyone who doubts this has only to ask his local newspaper or his congressman about the mail, a tremendous proportion of it anti-Negro, that has come in since the riots.

Another consequence was a perverse gain of one of the demands of the civil rights leaders. Commissioner Murphy changed his position and assigned a highly qualified Negro captain, Lloyd Sealy, to command the 28th Precinct. He became the first Negro to command a Harlem precinct. More Negro patrolmen and officers were also dispatched to the 28th and other Harlem precincts.

Another benefit was in the tangible separation of the men from the boys among the contenders for responsible Negro leadership. The distinction is quite simple: There were lots of leaders willing to speak *for* the mob, and few who had the courage to speak *to* the mob.

Of the latter, two alone stand out: Bayard Rustin, who had the moral strength to tell the Harlem mob to call him an Uncle Tom if it would save lives; and George Fleary, who, with fewer supporters, opposed the mob in Bedford-Stuyvesant. Three others deserve partial recognition: in Harlem, CORE's James Farmer and the Harlem Unity Committee's L. Joseph Overton; and in Brooklyn, the Reverend V. Simpson Turner, executive director of the Protestant Council's Brooklyn Division.

Even a leader takes his life in his hands when he speaks out against a mob in full swing. Stanley Branche, of the Chester, Pennsylvania, Committee for Freedom Now, one of the most successful civil rights spokesmen in the East, was hit by a brick when he tried to dissuade Philadelphia rioters. "When the slaves come up out of the galleys, they throw everybody overboard," Assemblyman Tom Jones says.

Some other leaders have begun to make capital of the rioting. The Reverend Milton Galamison, appearing on the WABC Press Conference after the riots, said:

"My answer is if one can't gain objectives through

207

mediation around the table, if one can't gain objectives through peaceful demonstrations and picketing, if one can't even gain objectives after a riot, then all these things may become a Sunday School picnic by comparison to what people are going to have to do in order to get their just grievances remedied."

The Harlem and Bedford-Stuyvesant riots of July are over, and remembering them is like remembering nightmares. A quick succession of violent images comes to mind: the Molotov cocktails; the police charges; the looting; the vandalism; the abuse, verbal and physical. And yet—much as in a nightmare—it is the incongruous that stands out in the memory. In Harlem, it was Sullivan's hospitable bar, an oasis of sanity in a desert of madness.

In Bedford-Stuyvesant it was the planes, sleek new jets, already high, but fighting for more altitude as the roar of their engines drowned out the curses and crashes of the rioting every half hour or so. The mobs on the street, the police, and the reporters would look up for an instant to watch them pass, their lights twinkling in the night sky, and then they'd be gone, north to Boston or Montreal. And then it came to mind that those who live in Bedford-Stuyvesant have to watch those jets passing far above them every few minutes, day and night, sleek symbols of a world they could only yearn for—or throw a brick at.

Appendix

At approximately 9:30 on the morning of July 16, 1964, James Powell, a fifteen year old boy, was shot to death by Lieutenant Thomas Gilligan, a New York City police officer. The office of the District Attorney of New York County immediately commenced an investigation. An exhaustive search for all possible witness was conducted.

On July 21st the Second July Grand Jury began hearing evidence presented by Assistant District Attorney Alexander Herman, Chief of the Homicide Bureau, and Assistant District Attorney Martin J. Heneghan. The jury held fifteen sessions and heard forty-five witnesses. Under the law, the testimony of these witnesses before the grand jury is secret. However, all known witnesses, including those referred to the office by various organizations, were interviewed by members of the District Attorney's staff.

The grand jury now has concluded that, on the basis

209

of the evidence and the applicable rules of law, Lieutenant Gilligan is not criminally liable for the killing of young Powell. In view of that determination and in light of the great public interest evinced in the case, the District Attorney's office has prepared this report, summarizing in detail what has been learned in the course of the investigation. Appended hereto is a statement of the controlling legal principles.

The Scene and the Incident Preceding the Shooting

Although there was disagreement among many of the witnesses with respect to the details of the shooting itself, there was substantial agreement concerning the essential facts of the incident which preceded the encounter of James Powell and Lieutenant Gilligan.

At about 9:15 on the morning of July 16, 1964, the superintendent of 215 East 76th Street and three other buildings on the block, had commenced his morning task of watering the flowers and plants in front of No. 211 and the two trees in front of No. 215. Across the street on the south side of the block, and somewhat east of No. 215, is the Robert Wagner Junior High School. As was common, a number of the summer session students—estimates ranged up to one hundred—were standing about on both sides of the street, leaning against cars, or sitting on stoops. Whether intentionally or not, the superintendent wet a few of the children who were in the immediate vicinity. Some of the youngsters then began throwing garbage can covers and bottles. One boy came at the superintendent with a lid in one hand and a bottle in the other. Dropping the hose, and running into No. 215, the superintendent was hit in the shoulder by the bottle, while the cover broke one of the panes of the outer door of the building.

No. 215 is an apartment building. Two steps, a total of ten and one-half inches in height, lead to the stoop landing, which is four feet three and one-half inches deep and four feet nine inches wide; another step leads to the outer door. On each side of the landing is a wall two feet four and one-half inches high topped by a railing two feet high. From the building line to the curb is a distance of fifteen feet two inches. On the west side of the stoop at No. 215 is a television service store and on the east side a cleaning store. Parked in front of the building that morning was the service truck of the TV store, and behind the truck a passenger car.

Medical and Ballistics Evidence

An autopsy was performed by a Deputy Chief Medical Examiner. Examination of the body showed that Powell was 5 feet 6½ inches tall and weighed 122 pounds. He had been struck by two bullets. One bullet entered the lower part of the right forearm, just above the back of the wrist and came out the other side. This bullet then pierced the deceased's chest above the right nipple, and came to rest in the left lung. Death as a result of this wound alone would have followed anytime within minutes to a half hour. The other bullet entered just above the navel to the left of center, and emerged at the opposite point in the back, having pierced the abdomen and a major vein. This wound could likewise have been fatal. There was no evidence on the body of smoke, flame or powder marks, thus indicating that both bullets must have travelled more than a foot and half before striking Powell.

A ballistics expert examined Powell's clothing in the hospital. There were no powder burns or scorch marks on the clothing, and, therefore, in his opinion, the gun

211

must have been farther than two feet from Powell's body when fired. A survey was made of the hallway of No. 215. Lodged in the jamb of the inner door, forty inches above the floor, was a deformed .38 caliber bullet. This bullet had first pierced a glass panel of the outer door, thirty-five inches above the floor. Thus, the bullet had been travelling at an upward angle. The position of the bullet and the depth of its penetration in the jamb, as well as the size and shape of the hole in the outer pane, nullified any possibility that it had first passed through Powell's body before reaching the hallway. The absence of any impact marks on the newly cemented sidewalk negated any possibility that Powell had been shot in the abdomen while lying on the ground.

Two of the bullets were too deformed for comparison. But ballistics tests of the bullet lodged in the chest proved that it had been fired from Gilligan's gun which, when examined, contained six cartridges, three discharged and three live.

The following day Gilligan was examined by a doctor, after having received first aid the day before at Roosevelt Hospital, where a splint had been applied to his right hand and forearm. The doctor diagnosed the injury as abrasion of the right upper forearm, superficial loss of skin on the right upper forearm, contusion and sprain of right hand and wrist, and recurrence of a previous sacroiliac injury resulting in a severe twisting of the back. The tissues of the right arm gave evidence of a sharp blow on the lateral margin of the right hand and forearm.

Students

Fifteen teen-agers, eight girls and seven boys, were questioned. Almost all had been friends of Powell, or had known him by name or sight; all, except one, were summer session students at the school.

Two boys, friends of the deceased, described his actions shortly preceding his encounter with Lieutenant Gilligan. That morning they had travelled with Powell from their homes in a housing project in the Bronx to the school. Powell showed them two knives, one with a red handle, the other black-handled, and let each of them keep one for him. After the superintendent had fled into the building, Powell crossed to the school side of the street and, according to the boy who had it, demanded the red-handled knife, stating, "I am going to cut that ***." The boy said he pretended not to have the knife. After some argument, Powell approached the other boy who said Powell asked for the black-handled knife, adding that he would be right back. The boy gave him the knife and, shortly thereafter, Powell was seen crossing the street, opening and closing the blade. A girl, who was following behind him, stated Powell told her that he was going to talk to the man. Pleading with him not to go, because there was liable to be trouble, she said she grabbed at him in an unsuccessful attempt to restrain him.

The recitals of what occurred at this point differ. The girl, who was following Powell and who had now stationed herself near the stoop, stated that he walked up the steps of No. 215, opened the door all the way, at which time Gilligan, coming from the direction of the TV store, stopped in front of the building, and, still on the sidewalk, shouted to Powell, causing him to turn around. Three students agreed with this account. But three other students claimed that Gilligan was already on the stoop facing the street, when Powell approached the building. Another three youngsters reported that both were on the sidewalk, facing each other in an east-west direction, when the shooting started. And, finally, two girls were positive that Gilligan followed Powell out of the building before he shot him.

In any event, several students recalled that the girl by the stoop yelled to Powell that the man had a gun. According to her, Powell, having turned around, then raised both hands whereupon Gilligan walked up the stoop and, approximately a foot and a half away from Powell, pushed his right hand. A boy, standing on the school side of the street said he also saw Gilligan grab at Powell's right hand, while others claimed that he turned the boy around so as to face him. A number of the students recounted that Powell was either waving or raising his arms, and one said he was flinging them as if to strike at the officer. None saw a knife in Powell's hand at this point, although one boy said he might have had a beer can in his hand, and one girl claimed that in fact he was holding a beer can in his right hand. Two students later saw a knife lying in the street near the curb.

Regardless of the nature of the encounter or the position of Powell and Gilligan, it was undisputed that a shot was soon fired. According to the girl by the stoop, the officer held his gun at waist level and fired one shot, causing Powell to fall to the sidewalk. Seven students only heard the first shot, their attention having been diverted, or their view having been blocked by other people or the parked vehicles; seven others simply stated that the officer fired a shot. One of the latter group expressly noted that the officer pointed the gun at Powell's right hand and then fired.

Almost all the students agreed that Powell fell after the first shot. According to the most frequent account, after Powell fell to the sidewalk on his hands and knees, the officer, still on the steps, pointed the gun down and fired two more shots at Powell's back. Two youngsters said Powell had first dropped to his knees clutching his abdomen. One girl was certain that Powell was lying on his back when Gilligan fired the final two shots down at him. Altogether, ten students reported that Gilligan fired two shots at Powell when he was down on the ground after having fallen from the first shot. But one of these witnesses was shown photographs of the hallway, proving a bullet had pierced a window of the outer door and had lodged in the jamb of the inner door. After looking at the photograph he said he was not sure of what he had seen. Upon further reflection he admitted that, in fact, he had not seen the shooting at all.

Of those who claimed to have seen the shooting, some acknowledged that their view was obstructed by the truck parked in front of No. 215, or by other children; some heard but did not see the last two shots; others admitted running for cover when the shooting started. All agreed that after the first shot there was a pause, then two shots in succession, and, finally, Powell lay flat on his stomach, body parallel with the curb, head towards Third Avenue, while Gilligan stood over him holding the gun pointed at the body. Many of the students claimed that Gilligan then either nudged or pushed or kicked Powell over onto his back. But when Powell's two friends, who had been holding the knives for him, ran over from the opposite side of the street, after having heard the three shots, Powell was still face down and Gilligan stood over him rubbing his fingers. The boy who had given Powell the knife asked Gilligan why he had shot him. Gilligan replied, "This is why," taking from his pocket a badge which he pinned

215

to his shirt. Asked why he didn't call an ambulance, Gilligan said that Powell was his prisoner and directed the boy to call the ambulance. The boy, who had refused to give Powell the red-handled knife, heard Gilligan say that Powell had tried to kill him and that he had a knife under him.

Adults

Various aspects of the events, prior to, during and subsequent to the shooting, were observed by eight passersby, two store owners, two neighborhood workmen, five teachers, and a priest. According to one of the owners of the TV store, Gilligan came in with a radio to be fixed and asked what was going on in the street. Told that the young people were just acting up, Gilligan remarked that he did not want to get involved in anything, that he wanted to his his radio fixed and leave. The shopkeeper saw the youths start throwing garbage can covers and soda bottles. There was a crash and he saw the superintendent run into the building. Gilligan then ran out the door.

Seven other people, a couple walking by the building, a practical nurse standing on the other side of the street, a truck driver walking to work, a bus driver on his way from work, the cleaning store owner, and a teacher looking out a third story school window, stated that Powell had run, leaped or swaggered onto the stoop, heading towards the entrance to number 215. Some saw Powell enter the building. Gilligan appeared from the direction of the TV store and, according to most versions, was standing on the sidewalk somewhere near the stoop when Powell started back down the stoop towards the street. Gilligan, according to the man in the television store, shouted, "Stop." Extending his left hand, he said, "I'm a lieutenant, drop it"; in his right hand he held a gun. Standing in the entranceway of the store, the owner looked to the doorway of the building and saw the head and shoulders of someone coming out in a crouched position, clenched hand raised to shoulder level. A bus driver standing near No. 209 said that Powell had a knife in his right hand and was moving off the stoop towards the officer, who was on the sidewalk facing the building. He related that Gilligan, holding a badge in his open palm, had shouted, "Stop, I'm a cop." An air conditioning mechanic, whose truck was halted by traffic about three buildings west of No. 215, heard someone shout, "Stop and drop it." From his elevated cab, he then saw Powell standing with one foot on the sidewalk and one foot on the bottom step of the stoop. Facing Powell, about two or three feet away was Gilligan. A knife in his right hand, the boy paused, raised it to about head level away from his body, and started to come down with it, striking at Gilligan. There was a shot. Powell started to slump but came up again. He raised the knife and again swung at Gilligan. There was another shot. Traffic started to move, and the witness drove away towards Second Avenue. A workman on a scaffold four buildings east of No. 215 looked in the direction of the building after the first shot. According to his version, Powell was moving rapidly and coming down from the stoop but still on the landing while Gilligan was on the sidewalk in front of the TV store. In his right hand Gilligan held some object and his left hand was partially outstretched. Powell, with his hands raised and fists clenched, also held an object in his hand. As he then climbed up the rope of the scaffold to safety, he heard two more shots.

Other witnesses differed concerning the positions of Gilligan and Powell. A truck driver, who was standing in front of the cleaning store insisted that Gilligan had followed Powell into the building and that they were both still in the hallway when the three shots were fired. Two witnesses maintained that one or all three shots were fired from the street into the hallway, while one passerby said Gilligan was in front of the TV store window when he fired toward the door. A teacher who was standing by a fourth story window when the first shot was fired thought that Gilligan was facing the street and Powell the building when the next two shots were fired.

All the witnesses who heard three shots, except one, agreed that the first shot was followed by a pause and then two shots in succession. All, who had seen Powell fall to the sidewalk, recalled that he did not reach the ground until all three shots had been fired. Powell lay on the sidewalk face down, while Gilligan stood over him, pointing his gun at him. The TV man heard the officer tell Powell not to move. Two teachers, looking from the third and fourth floor windows, respectively, claimed that Gilligan then pushed Powell over onto his back. A man standing by the cleaning store maintained, however, that an ambulance attendant turned over the body, and a man who had been working in a nearby building said that a clergyman and a police officer turned Powell over onto his back. But the priest who arrived on the scene stated that Powell was already on his back when he arrived. Two men heard Gilligan say that there was a knife under the boy. They also noticed a badge hanging from Gilligan's pants pocket.

Two other witnesses saw a knife in the street after the shooting. A young school teacher who lives in the neighborhood noticed a knife blade lying next to Powell's thigh, between his body and the stoop. While standing there she saw someone kick the knife toward the curb. A teacher who ran out of the school after the shooting saw a knife lying in the gutter about ten feet from Powell. The blade was open. He picked it up, closed it, and gave it to a police officer. Powell's young friend later identified this knife as the black-handled knife he had received from Powell and returned to him just before the shooting.

Police Officers

Several uniformed police officers arrived at the scene approximately 9:30. Two saw Powell lying face down with his left arm partly under his head. One of them turned Powell over in an attempt to administer first aid. The other officer was handed the black-handled knife by a teacher. Now in the District Attorney's custody, this knife, open, measures eight and seven-eighths inches. Its single blade is three and one-half inches long.

Statement of Lieutenant Gilligan

Lieutenant Gilligan is thirty-seven years old, has been a policeman for seventeen years. He is six feet, two inches tall, and weighs about two hundred pounds. Questioned extensively, Lieutenant Gilligan gave the following version of the events. July 16th was his day off. His radio having gone dead that morning, he decided to take it to the Jadco TV Service Company, located at 215 East 76th Street in the precinct where he formerly worked. Arriving at about 9:20 or 9:25 a.m., he noticed two groups of youngsters standing around a man who was hosing the sidewalk. Upon entering the store, he was told that there had been some trouble earlier and that the police had been called.

Suddenly, Gilligan heard the sound of breaking glass and saw people running in the street. Dropping the hose, the superintendent ran into the building. A boy, following behind, threw a bottle and garbage can cover at the man and ran away. Gilligan then stepped outside and spotted Powell running around the front of the parked service truck towards the building, yelling, "Hit him, hit him, hit him." In his right hand, held close to his chest, was an open knife, blade pointed down. Powell ran towards the hallway. Gilligan, removing his badge from his left trouser pocket and his revolver from his right pocket, moved to a point in front of the stoop, facing the building entrance. By this time Powell was just inside the hallway at the outer door. Holding the shield in his outstretched hand in front of him, Gilligan said, "I'm a police lieutenant. Come out and drop it." Looking over his shoulder, Powell glanced from the badge to the gun. Gilligan repeated the warning. Powell turned, raised the knife in front of his chest and lunged at the officer. Pointing the gun to his left, Gilligan fired a warning shot into the building and again told him to stop. Powell, now close to the edge of the stoop landing, struck at the officer with the knife. Gilligan blocked it with his right hand, which still held the gun, and attempted to push Powell back, but the knife scraped along his arm causing it to bleed and later to swell. Powell was bent back but again struck with the knife. This time Gilligan, who claims to be an expert shot, pointed his gun slightly upwards and fired at the raised hand, seeking to dislodge the knife. But Powell, still above the officer on the stoop, again lunged forward, knife hand pumping. Gilligan stepped back and fired into the boy's midsection. Powell staggered and collapsed onto the sidewalk, face down. The knife lay nearby. Gilligan backed around onto the stoop, holding the gun down by his side.

1. The killing of one human being by another is a criminal homicide, unless the act is "justifiable" or otherwise excused by law.

2. Deadly force is justifiable if used in self-defense, whether by a private citizen or a police officer. The theory of self-defense may be termed, "reasonably apparent necessity": deadly force is justified if the slayer has a reasonable basis, in all the circumstances, for believing at the moment of the slaying that such force is necessary to prevent imminent, grave personal injury to himself.

If James Powell did not attack Lt. Gilligan, or attacked him but without a dangerous weapon, and Gilligan had no reason for believing that he was in imminent danger, the shooting was not justified as self-defense. If Powell attacked Gilligan with a knife, but there was a reasonable alternative to shooting, Gilligan was obliged to make every effort, consistent with his own safety, to avoid the danger before using fatal force. He could shoot without retreating, however, if it was reasonable to believe at the moment of the attack that retreat was impossible or would have increased the danger. This is so even if, upon subsequent reflection, it appears that such belief was mistaken, and there was an opportunity to retreat without increasing the danger.

3. Deadly force is justifiable not only under the law of self-defense, but also under certain principles governing the use of force by a police officer in the performance of his duties.

At all times, a New York City policeman is required to carry his service revolver, and bound to protect life and property, prevent crime, and arrest offenders. If, while "off duty," Gilligan observed a public disturbance, he was obliged to intercede, and could arrest any person on reasonable grounds for believing that he was committing a crime or offense in the officer's presence. Homicide is justifiable when committed by a police officer in attempting lawfully to apprehend a person for a crime actually committed, when the circumstances are such that one would have reasonable cause for believing that the crime was a felony, and that deadly force is necessary to apprehend the suspect. Assault with a knife, and assaulting a police officer with intent to resist lawful arrest, are felonies.

Therefore, if Gilligan was acting as a police officer, and lawfully attempting to apprehend Powell for some crime or offense committed in his presence, such as possession of a knife with intent to use it unlawfully upon another, or disorderly conduct, and Powell resisted arrest by assaulting Gilligan in any manner, this assault was a felony; if Powell assaulted Gilligan with a dangerous weapon, a separate felony was committed. The officer was then entitled to use deadly force to apprehend Powell, but only if he had a reasonable basis for believing that such force was necessary.

4. The presumption of innocence applies in the grand jury room. The grand jury ought to find an indictment only when all the evidence before them, taken together, is such as in their judgment would, if unexplained or uncontradicted, warrant a conviction by a trial jury by a verdict of guilty beyond a reasonable doubt. The grand jury should consider all the evidence, and where there appear irreconcilable discrepancies, the grand jury should resolve issues of credibility.

Thus, no indictment could be found against Lt. Gilligan unless at least twelve of the grand jurors concluded that a petit jury would be persuaded by the evidence that, beyond a reasonable doubt, the killing was unjustified.